South Your Mouth

South Your Mouth

Tried & True Southern Recipes

Mandy Rivers

QUAIL RIDGE PRESS

Preserving America's Food Heritage

To Jeff, for believing enough for both of us.

First edition, July 2014

Back cover photo of Mandy Rivers by Beth Palfrey
Food photography by Mandy Rivers

ISBN 978-1-938879-01-2
Manufactured in the United States of America

QUAIL RIDGE PRESS
P. O. Box 123 • Brandon, MS 39043 • 1-800-343-1583
info@quailridge.com • www.quailridge.com

Contents

Acknowledgments

Thank you to Barney and Gwen McKee for believing in me and supporting this cookbook, and for their invaluable help in the development process.

This book is my lovechild with Terresa Sullivan, Melinda Burnham, Cyndi Clark, Holly Hardy, and Lacy Ward of Quail Ridge Press. Without their hard work and wicked awesome publishing skills, there would be no book at all!

I would like to thank my food blog buddies who have helped and inspired me along the way: Brandie Skibinski, Christy Jordan, Stacey Little, Mary Foreman, and Kris Meyer.

Thanks to the friends who've been my sisters when I had none.

I love you, Mom and Dad, for raising me right. For making me work hard. For always making sure I had what I needed, not necessarily what I wanted. For your unwavering, constant devotion, love and support.

And there aren't enough expressions or gestures or words to express my gratitude to my incredible husband Jeff and my sweet, sweet children and the incredible journey of a life we have. I love you more than I know how to tell you.

Preface

If you were to come over to my house, I would pour you a glass of something cold to drink, ask you if you were hungry (then feed you anyway regardless of your answer, because that's what we do here in the South), invite you to sit on my screened porch, turn on the ceiling fan to make sure you were cool enough, and then we'd swap stories about our days and our lives. When you read this book, you'll be right there on my porch with me laughing about my crazy life and enjoying the food that brings me so much joy. I've yet to meet a stranger, so I'm going to call you friend and, friend, I'm glad you're here . . . and I hope you enjoy your time here with me.

There is a story to be told behind every great recipe. Writing my South Your Mouth blog has been as much about documenting recipes as it has been about telling my story. Day by day. Recipe by recipe.

I am a food writer and recipe creator, but I am also a mother of three amazing little people, a wife to a man who loves me more than I deserve, a daughter to two parents who have loved me every day of my life and made sure I never went without anything I needed, and a friend to some of the most colorful, interesting, thoughtful people imaginable . . . and I bring all parts of myself to my recipes and stories.

If you don't already follow my blog, I'd love for you to visit me there, and get to know me better. Just think of me as your southern neighbor, and drop by any time you're hungry or just need to laugh. I'm so tickled you're reading my very first cookbook, and I hope you enjoy my recipes and stories as much as I have enjoyed sharing them with you.

Peace and bacon grease,

Mandy

Baked Pimento Cheese Dip

Beverages & Appetizers

Never go grocery shopping when you're hungry. The last time I did, I bought two pounds of Cheddar cheese. I got home and thought, now, what are you going to do with that mammoth-sized block of cheese? So I did what any good southerner would do . . . I made Pimento Cheese Spread!

Southern Brewed Sweet Tea

1 gallon water, divided

4 family-size or 8 regular-size tea bags

1½–2 cups sugar, or to taste

Lemon slices (optional)

Fill a pot with 2 quarts of cold water, and bring to a boil. Remove from heat, add tea bags, and steep tea for 1–2 hours. Remove tea bags. Add tea and sugar to a gallon-size pitcher, and stir until sugar has dissolved. Add remaining 2 quarts of water, and stir well. Refrigerate until cold before serving. Serve with lemon, if desired.

Banana Shimmies

It's not quite a shake, so I call it a shimmy. The combination of rich whole milk and the creamy banana makes for quite a velvety, rich, frosty treat.

1 medium-size ripe banana, sliced

1 cup whole milk

1–2 packets Splenda, or to taste

Drop of vanilla extract

½ cup crushed ice

Add banana, milk, sweetener, and a drop of vanilla extract to a blender, and whip for about 30 seconds. Add ice, and blend for 10–20 seconds, or until smooth. Pour and enjoy! Makes 2 (8-ounce) servings.

Autumn Apple Buckle

Here's a quick cocktail recipe for your autumn libations. Cheers, y'all!

1 part vanilla vodka

1 part apple cider

2 parts ginger ale

Apple slices

Mix vodka, cider, and ginger ale, and serve over ice, or shake with ice to serve martini-style. Garnish with apple slices.

Creamsicle Crush

Y'all, this whipped cream vodka is so good!

3 ounces whipped cream vodka

3 ounces orange juice

2 ounces whole milk or half-and-half

1 teaspoon powdered sugar

1 cup crushed ice

Add all ingredients to a cocktail shaker. Cover tightly, and shake vigorously. Pour into powdered-sugar rimmed glass, and serve. To rim the glass, pour ⅛ of an inch of vodka into a small saucer. Add ½ cup powdered sugar to another saucer. Turn a tall glass upside down into the vodka to coat the rim then dip the glass into the sugar, rolling it around a bit until the rim is thoroughly coated.

Summer Citrus Sangria

1 ruby red grapefruit, washed, halved

1 lime, washed, sliced

1 orange, washed, sliced

1 lemon, washed, sliced

1¼ cups sugar, or to taste

1 cup orange vodka

1 bottle Chardonnay

1 (12-ounce) can lemon-lime soda

Juice half the grapefruit, and add juice to a 2-quart pitcher. Slice the remaining grapefruit half, and add with other fruit slices, sugar, and vodka to pitcher; stir until sugar is dissolved. Refrigerate for at least 4 hours (or overnight). When ready to serve, add Chardonnay and lemon-lime soda. Serve over ice, if desired.

Tennessee Honey Hole

This is light, bubbly, and fresh from the peaches and soda, but somehow rich and decadent at the same time from the whiskey and honey. It's super easy, and it's to die for in iced tea!

Diced fresh peaches

1 ounce peach syrup (such as Monin's)

2 ounces Jack Daniel's Tennessee Honey

2 ounces ginger ale

Place a scant handful of peaches and peach syrup in the bottom of a highball glass. Using the handle of a wooden spoon, muddle peaches in syrup (smash them up a bit). Fill glass with ice, then add Jack Daniels Tennessee Honey and ginger ale. Stir, then serve.

Eggnog Latte

This tastes EXACTLY like the latte I got at the coffee shop for $5.00. Except it's not actually a latte, since I don't have a milk steamer, but whatever . . . latte sounds so much better than coffee, so just go with it.

⅔ cup eggnog

⅓ cup milk

Sugar to taste

2 shots espresso, or ½ cup double strength coffee

Whipped cream and nutmeg (optional)

Mix eggnog and milk in a large mug, and microwave for 1 minute or more till very hot. Add sugar to taste, and stir well. Holding the espresso as far above the mug as you dare, pour espresso into eggnog mixture (this creates a little foam—holla!). Top with whipped cream and freshly grated nutmeg, if desired.

Homemade Salsa

Y'all! This is amazing and so easy to prepare. It looks like the salsa you get in Mexican restaurants around here, but it has so much more flavor.

2 (28-ounce) cans whole tomatoes, drained, divided

1 bunch cilantro

1–2 jalapeño peppers, roughly chopped

6–7 cloves garlic

½ onion, roughly chopped

1 teaspoon cumin

1 teaspoon salt

½ teaspoon pepper

Juice of 1 lime (optional)

Add approximately half of the tomatoes to a food processor (or blender). Cut the bare stems off the cilantro, and add leaves to the food processor. Add jalapeños, garlic, and onion to the food processor, and pulse until there are no large chunks remaining, 5–6 times. Add remaining ingredients, and pulse 2–3 times or until you reach the consistency you like. Refrigerate until ready to serve.

Cool Ranch Spinach Dip

This is one of my most favorite dips!

- **1 (10-ounce) box frozen chopped spinach, thawed**
- **1 (8-ounce) can sliced water chestnuts, drained**
- **8 ounces sour cream**
- **1 packet ranch dressing mix (not dip mix)**

Strain all water from spinach by pressing into a colander or wringing out by hand. Add strained spinach to a mixing bowl. Dice water chestnuts, and add to spinach. Add sour cream and ranch dressing mix, and stir until all ingredients are thoroughly combined. Cover, and refrigerate until ready to serve.

Creamy Crack Dip

It's so good, it's addictive!

- **1 pound pork sausage (mild or hot)**
- **2 (8-ounce) packages cream cheese, at room temperature**
- **2 (10-ounce) cans diced tomatoes and green chiles, well drained**
- **½ teaspoon garlic salt**

Brown sausage, then drain grease. Combine with remaining ingredients in a slow cooker. Heat until bubbly, stirring occasionally. Keep warm, and serve with tortilla chips.

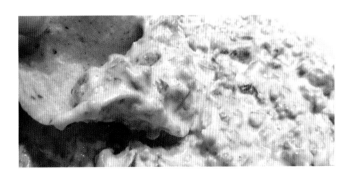

Homemade French Onion Dip

Now that I've made this from scratch, I will never, ever buy French onion dip again. So easy and so incredibly delicious!

2 very large yellow onions, chopped

¼ cup butter

1 tablespoon vegetable oil

1½ teaspoons salt

1 teaspoon sugar

2 teaspoons Worcestershire

½ teaspoon dried thyme (or 1 tablespoon fresh)

3 cloves garlic, minced

1 (16-ounce) container sour cream

Add chopped onions, butter, vegetable oil, salt, and sugar to a large skillet, and cook, uncovered, over medium heat for 20 minutes, stirring occasionally. Add Worcestershire, thyme, and garlic, and continue cooking over medium heat for about 20 minutes, until onions are caramelized and deep golden brown in color. Remove from heat, and cool to room temperature.

In a serving bowl, combine sour cream and caramelized onions, and mix well. Cover, and refrigerate until ready to serve. Serve with crackers, chips, pretzels, and/or chopped fresh vegetables.

Homemade French Onion Dip

Pimento Cheese Spread

Never go grocery shopping when you're hungry. The last time I did, I bought two pounds of Cheddar cheese. I got home and thought, now, what are you going to do with that mammoth-sized block of cheese? So I did what any good southerner would do . . . I made Pimento Cheese Spread!

1 pound Cheddar cheese (medium or sharp)

1 cup mayonnaise

½ teaspoon salt

⅛ teaspoon cayenne pepper

⅛ teaspoon white pepper

⅛ teaspoon onion powder

⅛ teaspoon granulated garlic

1 (4-ounce) jar pimentos, drained well

Shred cheese, then add to a large mixing bowl; set aside. Combine mayonnaise, salt, cayenne pepper, white pepper, onion powder, and garlic; mix well. Add mayo mixture and drained pimentos to shredded cheese, and stir until all ingredients are thoroughly incorporated. Add more mayo, if desired. Refrigerate until ready to serve.

Baked Pimento Cheese Dip

After I made way too much pimento cheese, I decided to use it to try something new . . . Baked Pimento Cheese. It turned out FABULOUS!

8–10 slices bacon

1 pound Cheddar cheese (medium or sharp)

1 (4-ounce) jar pimentos, drained well

1 cup mayonnaise

½ teaspoon salt

¼ teaspoon cayenne pepper

½ teaspoon granulated garlic

1 bunch green onions, diced

1 cup crushed Ritz Crackers

Cut bacon into ½-inch pieces, then cook until crispy. Drain on paper towels. Set aside.

Shred cheese into a medium-size mixing bowl. Add cooked bacon, pimentos, mayonnaise, salt, cayenne pepper, and garlic; mix well until all ingredients are thoroughly incorporated. Fold in green onions.

Spread cheese mixture evenly into a 8x10-inch baking dish. Bake at 350° for 20 minutes. Sprinkle crushed crackers evenly on top of cheese, and return dish to oven. Bake 20 more minutes, or until crackers are golden brown and cheese is bubbly. Serve with crackers and/or celery sticks.

Peanut Butter Cream Pie Dip

1 (14-ounce) can sweetened
   condensed milk

1 (8-ounce) block cream
   cheese, at room temperature

1 cup peanut butter

1 cup powdered sugar

1 (8-ounce) carton Cool Whip,
   thawed, divided

Chocolate graham crackers or
   chocolate wafers

Combine sweetened condensed milk and cream cheese, and beat with an electric mixer on medium speed until smooth. Add peanut butter and powdered sugar, and mix until blended. Add half of Cool Whip, and mix until smooth. Fold in remaining Cool Whip, and mix until just combined. Serve with chocolate graham crackers or chocolate wafers.

Key Lime Pie Dip

This recipe quickly went to the top of my blog stats for the week, and blew up Pinterest.

1 (14-ounce) can sweetened
   condensed milk

1 (8-ounce) block cream
   cheese, at room temperature

⅔ cup fresh lime juice

1 tablespoon lime zest

1 cup powdered sugar

1 (8-ounce) carton Cool Whip,
   thawed

Graham crackers for dipping

Combine sweetened condensed milk and cream cheese, and beat with an electric mixer on medium speed until smooth. Add lime juice, zest, and powdered sugar, and mix until blended. Fold in Cool Whip, and mix until just combined. Add mixture to a serving bowl, and refrigerate for 4 hours. Garnish with a slice of lime, if desired. Serve with graham crackers.

NOTE:
To make Key Lime Pies, fill 2 standard graham cracker pie crusts.

Caramel Apple Dip

I've never had anything like this. The caramel is beyond rich and creamy, and then there's the crunch from the toffee bits, and it all meets up with the crisp, tart apple! Stop it! Just stop it!

8 ounces cream cheese, softened

¾ cup packed brown sugar

½ cup sugar

1 teaspoon vanilla extract

1 (14-ounce) container caramel dip (usually found in the produce section)

1 (8-ounce) bag toffee bits (such as Heath's Bits 'O Brickle)

Beat cream cheese with an electric mixer on medium speed until smooth. Add brown sugar, sugar, vanilla, and caramel dip, then continue mixing until thoroughly combined. Stir in toffee bits by hand. Refrigerate in an airtight container until ready to serve. Serve with apple slices.

TIP:
To keep apple slices from browning, toss them with lemon juice.

Ham and Cheddar Roll-Ups

Ham and Cheddar Roll-Ups

The Honey Butter Dipping Sauce is so good, it nearly knocked my socks off!

1 (8-ounce) can crescent rolls

1 cup finely shredded Cheddar cheese

24 thin slices smoked ham

HONEY BUTTER DIPPING SAUCE:

3 tablespoons honey

3 tablespoons butter

3 tablespoons yellow mustard

Line a baking sheet with aluminum foil, and lightly spray with cooking spray. Separate crescent rolls into dough triangles. Sprinkle cheese on each triangle. Folding ham slices to fit, arrange 3 slices of ham on each triangle. Starting at the wide end, roll triangles, and place each roll-up on the cooking sheet with the end point of the dough tucked under the roll-up (to prevent it from opening up during cooking). Bake at 375° for 11–12 minutes.

Whisk honey, butter, and mustard in a microwave-safe bowl, and microwave for 20 seconds; whisk until smooth. (You may have to microwave for an additional 20 seconds if the mixture doesn't whisk together smoothly.)

Holiday Ham Rolls

24 sweet Hawaiian rolls

1 pound sliced honey ham

½ pound sliced Swiss cheese

½ cup butter, melted

2 tablespoons Dijon mustard

2 tablespoons poppy seeds

1 teaspoon Worcestershire

Slice rolls in half using a serrated knife. Arrange bottom halves of rolls in a large glass baking dish, and top with ham and cheese. Replace top halves of rolls. In a medium bowl, mix remaining ingredients until well combined. Drizzle honey mustard sauce over top of the rolls. Cover with aluminum foil, and allow to sit for at least 1 hour (or in refrigerator overnight). Bake at 350° for 20–25 minutes or until the cheese is melted. Serve warm or at room temperature.

Queso Roll-Ups

2 (8-ounce) packages cream cheese, softened

1 (1-ounce) package taco seasoning

6 (10-inch) flour tortillas

1 (10-ounce) can diced tomatoes and green chiles, drained well

2–3 cups finely shredded Mexican blend cheese

With an electric mixer, beat cream cheese on medium speed until fluffy. Add taco seasoning, and mix well. Spread each tortilla with cream cheese mixture. Sprinkle tortillas with diced tomatoes, then top with shredded cheese.

Roll each tortilla very tightly, then roll in plastic wrap. Refrigerate for 4–6 hours. When ready to serve, slice into pinwheels.

Naked Chicken Tenders

I use my chicken seasoning (Chicken Scratch) each and every time I cook chicken. Whether I'm baking it, grilling it, frying it, sautéing it, or putting it in ice cream, it gets a good coating of seasoning!

1 pound chicken breast tenderloins

1–2 tablespoons Chicken Scratch (see page 112)

3–4 tablespoons vegetable oil

Season tenderloins with Chicken Scratch. Heat vegetable oil in a large skillet over medium-high heat, using enough oil to completely cover bottom of skillet. Once oil is hot, place about half the tenderloins in skillet. (Do not overcrowd pan.) Cook about 4 minutes, or until lightly browned on each side, then remove from heat. Repeat with remaining chicken tenders. Let rest about 10 minutes before serving. I mean it!

Original Sausage Balls

I knew what went into sausage balls, but I didn't know how much because I'd never made them. I hopped online to find the recipe. You know, THE recipe? Because there's only one, right? Nope! There's like 40-gozillion recipes out there for sausage balls. This is what I came up with—so now there's 40-gozillion plus one. But mine is the best!

3 cups Bisquick baking mix

1 pound hot pork sausage

16 ounces shredded sharp Cheddar cheese (4 cups)

¼ cup chopped fresh chives or parsley (optional)

Combine all ingredients, and mix at low speed using the paddle attachment (or mix by hand) until all ingredients are evenly combined. Roll dough into 1½-inch balls, and place on a baking sheet 1 inch apart. (I used my handy-dandy cookie scoop to make quick work out of portioning these.) Bake at 350° for 20–25 minutes or until lightly browned on the bottom.

Mozzarella-Stuffed Meatballs

As I was pilfering through my scantily stocked refrigerator (because I needed to go grocery shopping and couldn't make the time!), I came across the cheese sticks I pack in my kids' lunchboxes. And the wheels started turning . . . .

1½ pounds ground beef

2 eggs, beaten

1 tablespoon Italian seasoning

¾ teaspoon salt

¾ teaspoon black pepper

¾ teaspoon garlic powder

Pinch of red pepper flakes

¼ cup grated Parmesan cheese

⅓ cup Italian dried bread crumbs

3 (1-ounce) individually-wrapped mozzarella cheese sticks

In a bowl, combine ground beef, eggs, Italian seasoning, salt, pepper, garlic, and red pepper, using your hands to mix until just combined. (Don't squeeze; just combine, as overworking the meat is what yields that "corky" texture.) Add Parmesan and bread crumbs; continue to mix with your hands until just combined.

Turn mixture onto a cutting board or clean counter; shape into a rectangle. Pat down good, and keep working on it until it's perfectly shaped. Using a sharp knife, cut mixture into 24 squares.

Line a baking sheet with aluminum foil (for easy cleanup), and spray with cooking spray; set aside.

Cut each cheese stick into 8 pieces (24 pieces total); press 1 into center of each meatball square. Roll each square into tight ball. Place meatballs onto baking sheet; bake at 400° for 15–18 minutes. Don't overcook, or the mozzarella might bubble out. Serve immediately.

Deviled Eggs

6 large eggs

⅓ cup mayonnaise, or to taste

½ teaspoon yellow mustard

½ teaspoon Dijon mustard

Salt to taste

Paprika and/or chopped chives (optional)

Cover eggs with cold water by at least an inch in a medium saucepan. Bring water to a full rolling boil; boil eggs 1 minute. Cover pan, and remove from heat. Let eggs stand in hot water, covered, 20 minutes. Pour off water, and refill pan with cold water and a few cups of ice. Let eggs sit for 10 minutes.

Peel eggs; cut in half lengthwise. Add yolks to small bowl; arrange egg whites on a serving dish. Add mayonnaise and mustards to egg yolks, and mash together. Add salt to taste, and more mayonnaise, if needed, to reach desired consistency. Using electric mixer, whip yolk mixture until smooth. Add to a piping bag or zip-top bag with a small hole cut in one corner, and pipe mixture into egg whites.

Refrigerate until ready to serve. Garnish with paprika and/or chopped chives, if desired.

Southern Cheddar Pecan Wafers

¾ cup all-purpose flour

1 teaspoon salt

½ teaspoon cayenne pepper

¼ teaspoon black pepper

2 cups grated sharp Cheddar cheese

¼ cup butter, at room temperature

¾ cup chopped pecans

Coarse-grain salt

In a small bowl, stir together flour, salt, cayenne pepper, and black pepper. Set aside. With an electric mixer, combine the cheese and butter until well blended. Add the flour mixture and pecans; beat on low speed until thoroughly incorporated. The dough should be fairly stiff, with small chunks of cheese and pecans visible. Transfer the dough to parchment paper, wax paper, or plastic wrap, and shape into a log about 1 inch in diameter. Wrap well, and freeze for 2 hours.

Grease a baking sheet or line with parchment paper. Unwrap the log, and cut into thin slices (no bigger than ¼ inch thick). Arrange the crackers on the baking sheet about 1 inch apart. Sprinkle with coarse-grain salt. Bake 7–10 minutes at 400° (depending on size and thickness), until bottoms start to brown.

Caramel Corn Snack Mix

This is SUCH a fun recipe for kids! I'm not sure which my kids like better—actually eating popcorn or helping me make it. They just squeal when (I totally let) a few pieces of popcorn escape and explode all over the kitchen.

8 cups popped plain popcorn

1 cup mini pretzels

1 cup salted nuts

½ cup (1 stick) salted butter

1 cup packed brown sugar

¼ cup corn syrup

½ teaspoon baking soda

Add popcorn, pretzels, and nuts to a standard-size brown grocery bag. Fold bag closed, and shake gently to combine ingredients. Set aside. Spray a large baking sheet with cooking spray. Set aside.

Melt butter in a medium pan over medium heat. Mix in brown sugar and corn syrup, and continue cooking until mixture begins to boil; boil for 2 minutes. Remove from heat, and immediately add baking soda. Stir until mixture begins to foam (less than 1 minute).

Pour caramel over popcorn mixture in brown bag. Fold bag closed again, and shake until popcorn mixture is evenly coated. Pour evenly onto baking sheet. Bake at 200° for 1 hour.

Remove caramel corn from oven, and cool completely. Store in an airtight container.

Bread & Breakfast

My children (I call them the onions) love those breakfast corndogs made with sausage and pancake batter. So I thought I'd try to make my own in mini muffin tins, and just pop them in the freezer, and pull out a few each morning as needed. Oh yeah!

Cheese Muffins

These are light and fluffy and cheesy . . . and really pretty unique.

1¾ cups all-purpose flour

1 tablespoon baking powder

½ teaspoon salt

2 tablespoons sugar

¾ cup grated sharp Cheddar cheese

1 egg

1 cup milk

¼ cup butter, melted

Combine flour, baking powder, salt, and sugar in a medium-large bowl, and stir to incorporate. Add cheese, and stir to combine. In a separate bowl, combine egg, milk, and butter, and mix well. Add egg mixture to flour mixture, and stir until just combined. Spoon mixture into a greased muffin tin, filling each muffin cup about ⅔ full. Bake at 400° for 20–25 minutes or until toothpick inserted in center comes out clean. Makes 10–12 muffins.

Raisin and Bran Muffins

2½ cups all-purpose flour

2½ teaspoons baking soda

1 teaspoon salt

2 eggs

1 teaspoon vanilla extract

½ cup butter (1 stick), melted

1½ cups sugar

2 cups buttermilk

½ cup raisins

2½ cups raisin and bran cereal

Sift together flour, baking soda, and salt; set aside. Cream eggs, vanilla, butter, and sugar with an electric mixer until creamy. Add buttermilk then flour mixture, and mix until just combined. Stir in raisins and raisin bran cereal. Line muffin tin with liners, or grease and flour each. Fill each ¾ full, then bake at 400° for 15–20 minutes, until toothpick inserted in the middle comes out clean. Cool completely, then store in airtight container.

Cheese Muffins

Chunky Monkey Muffins

So, I'm looking at four ripe bananas and thinking that I NEED to make something with these, when I spied a box of golden butter cake mix. The results? Easy, chunky, chewy, moist muffins!

4 ripe bananas

½ cup butter, softened

2 eggs

1 teaspoon vanilla

½ cup milk

½ cup sugar

½ teaspoon cinnamon

1 golden butter cake mix

1½ cups chopped pecans

2 cups shredded coconut

24 cupcake liners

Mix bananas, butter, eggs, and vanilla in a large bowl with a mixer on medium speed for 1 minute. Add milk, sugar, and cinnamon, and continue mixing for 1 additional minute. Add cake mix, and beat until just combined. Fold in pecans and coconut. Line 2 muffin tins with 24 cupcake liners, and divide batter evenly into each. Bake at 350° for 20–25 or until toothpick inserted in the center comes out clean.

Good Ol' Banana Bread

3–4 ripe bananas

½ cup vegetable oil

2 eggs

1 teaspoon vanilla extract

1 cup sugar

2 cups all-purpose flour

1 tablespoon baking soda

1 cup chopped pecans or walnuts (optional)

Peel and slice bananas, then add to a medium bowl. Using an electric mixer, beat bananas on low speed until creamy and only small chunks remain. Add oil, eggs, vanilla, and sugar, beating on low until well combined. Add flour and baking soda, and beat on low for 1–2 minutes, or until well combined. Stir in nuts, if desired.

Pour batter into a greased and floured loaf pan; bake at 350° for 45–50 minutes, or until toothpick inserted in middle comes out clean. Cool in pan for 20 minutes, then turn out and serve. Store at room temperature in an airtight container.

Twice as Nice Poppy Seed Bread

3 cups all-purpose flour

1½ teaspoons baking soda

1 teaspoon salt

2 cups sugar

1½ cups vegetable oil

2 eggs

1 (12-ounce) can evaporated milk

1½ teaspoons vanilla extract

¼ cup poppy seeds

1 cup chopped black walnuts

Sift together flour, baking soda, and salt; set aside. Mix sugar, oil, eggs, milk, and vanilla with an electric mixer until creamy. Add flour mixture and poppy seeds, and mix until combined. Stir in walnuts.

Grease and flour 2 standard-size loaf pans, then divide batter evenly into pans. Bake at 350° for 1 hour, or until toothpick inserted in the middle comes out clean. Serve warm. Or cool completely. Store in an airtight container.

Easy Cream Cheese Danish

1 (8-ounce) package cream cheese, at room temperature

½ cup sugar

1½ teaspoons lemon juice

½ teaspoon vanilla extract

2 (8-ounce) cans crescent rolls

1 cup powdered sugar

1 tablespoon milk

With electric mixer, combine cream cheese, sugar, lemon juice, and vanilla until fluffy; set aside.

Using a sharp knife, slice dough into ¾-inch slices, as if cutting slice-and-bake cookie dough. Place dough rounds 2 inches apart on ungreased baking sheet. Make a small well in the center of each. Spoon cream cheese mixture evenly into the wells of the dough. Bake, uncovered, at 350° for 15 minutes or until light golden brown. Combine powdered sugar and milk to make a glaze. Add more milk, if necessary, to reach desired consistency. Drizzle glaze over danishes to serve. Store in an airtight container once cooled.

Awesome Buttermilk Pancakes

Pancakes freeze beautifully between layers of wax paper. Reheat in the microwave for 20–30 seconds, or until heated through.

1 cup all-purpose flour

1 teaspoon baking powder

½ teaspoon baking soda

½ teaspoon salt

¾ cup buttermilk

1 egg, beaten

2 tablespoons melted butter

Vegetable oil

Combine dry ingredients in a medium bowl. In separate bowl, whisk together remaining ingredients except oil, then add to flour mixture. Whisk until just combined and most lumps are gone (do not overwork the batter).

Heat a large skillet over medium to medium-high heat. Drizzle skillet with vegetable oil. Pour portions of batter onto skillet (about ⅓ cup). Flip once, when bubbles can be seen in center of pancake and edges are golden brown. Continue cooking on other side until cooked through.

Cheddar Garlic Drop Biscuits

The secret to these biscuits is to use cold butter.

2 cups all-purpose flour

1 tablespoon baking powder

½ teaspoon salt

¼ teaspoon garlic powder

½ cup cold butter

1 cup whole milk

1 cup grated Cheddar cheese

GARLIC BUTTER TOPPING:

3 tablespoons butter, melted

½ teaspoon garlic powder

¼ teaspoon parsley

Pinch of salt

Combine flour, baking powder, salt, and garlic powder in a medium bowl; mix well. Using a cheese grater, grate cold butter into flour mixture. Gently stir with fork so butter is coated with flour and evenly distributed. Add milk and cheese, and stir until just combined (mixture will be sticky, but if it won't come together, add more flour, 1 tablespoon at a time). Spray a baking sheet with cooking spray. Drop ¼ cups of dough onto baking sheet 2–3 inches apart (I use an ice cream scoop). Bake at 400° for 14–16 minutes, until biscuits are lightly browned. While biscuits are baking, make Garlic Butter Topping.

Combine topping ingredients. Brush hot biscuits with topping, and serve immediately.

Cat Head Biscuits

A "cat head" is what we southerners call a big ol' biscuit (about the size of a cat's head).

3 cups all-purpose flour

1 tablespoon baking powder

½ teaspoon baking soda

1 teaspoon salt

¾ cup lard or shortening at room temperature

1¼ cups buttermilk

Melted butter

Generously grease a 9-inch cake pan with lard or shortening; set aside. Sift together flour, baking powder, baking soda, and salt into a large bowl. Cut lard or shortening into flour mixture with a fork or pastry cutter (or pulse in a food processor) until mixture is the consistency of coarse meal. Gently stir in buttermilk until just combined (do not overwork the dough). Portion dough into 6–8 biscuits, and place evenly into the prepared pan; biscuits will be touching. Brush biscuit tops with melted butter, and bake, uncovered, at 425° for 20 minutes or until fluffy and golden brown.

Hush Puppies

My son loves him some hush puppies. When he was about four years old, he strolled into the kitchen, scratching his head and asked me, "Mama, what's those little breads I like called . . . 'Quiet Doggies' or something like that?"

1¾ cups self-rising cornmeal

½ cup self-rising flour

1 teaspoon seasoned salt

2 teaspoons sugar

2 eggs, slightly beaten

1 cup buttermilk

2 tablespoons melted bacon grease

1 small onion, minced

Oil or shortening for frying

NOTE:
May substitute melted butter for bacon grease.

Heat a minimum of 4 inches of oil in a deep skillet to 350° over medium-high heat.

Mix cornmeal, flour, seasoned salt, and sugar in a medium bowl. In a separate bowl, combine eggs, buttermilk, and bacon grease (or butter), and mix well. Slowly add wet ingredients and minced onion to cornmeal mixture, stirring by hand. Stir until just combined.

Drop heaping teaspoonfuls of batter into hot grease. Cook Hush Puppies until golden brown (4–5 minutes), turning once. Hush Puppies will often flip over on their own when the bottom side is ready.

Skillet Cornbread

Skillet Cornbread

You may wonder why there's buttermilk and regular milk in this recipe. I've often wondered how things would be if I used all buttermilk, but since this is my mama's recipe, and it's absolutely perfect to me, I've never risked changing it!

2–3 tablespoons bacon grease

1 cup cornmeal (not self-rising)

½ cup all-purpose flour

1 tablespoon baking powder

1 teaspoon salt

½ teaspoon baking soda

1 cup buttermilk

½ cup milk

1 egg, well beaten

¼ cup vegetable oil

1 tablespoon sugar

Preheat oven to 450°. Add enough bacon grease to coat the bottom and side of 8- to 10-inch cast-iron skillet; place in hot oven while you make your batter. Combine cornmeal, flour, baking powder, salt, and baking soda in a medium bowl; stir to combine. In another bowl, combine buttermilk, milk, egg, vegetable oil, and sugar, and mix well. Stir in dry ingredients, and mix until just combined. Batter will be thin. Remove skillet from oven, and immediately pour batter into pan. Bake at 450° until browned around the edges (10–14 minutes). Remove from oven, and serve while hot.

NOTE:
Substitute vegetable oil for bacon grease, if necessary, then ask the Lord for forgiveness for throwing away your bacon grease. I mean it!

Mama's Cornbread Dressing

Down South, we make our dressing with cornbread. But since my mama's not a native southerner, she came up with a compromise that everyone loves by adding a little traditional packaged stuffing mix to the cornbread. And it's AH-MAZE-ING!

1 pan Skillet Cornbread (see page 40)

1 (14-ounce) bag herb stuffing

½ cup butter, plus more for greasing the pan

1 large onion, diced

1½ cups diced celery

Salt and pepper to taste

1 teaspoon dried sage, or to taste

4 cups chicken or turkey broth

Crumble cornbread into pieces the same size as the herb stuffing. Add to a large bowl; set aside.

Melt butter in a large skillet over medium-high heat; add onion and celery, and sauté 4–5 minutes. Add vegetables to cornbread mixture, along with salt, pepper, sage, and broth; gently toss until just combined. (Don't overmix the dressing, or you'll end up with a dense loaf.) Taste for seasoning at this point, and add more, if needed. Spoon dressing into a buttered 9x13-inch casserole dish. Bake, uncovered, at 350° for 30–40 minutes.

Sausage Corndog Muffins

My children (I call them the onions) love those breakfast corndogs made with sausage and pancake batter. So I thought I'd try to make my own in mini muffin tins, and just pop them in the freezer, and pull out a few each morning as needed. Oh yeah!

8 links maple-flavored breakfast sausage

1 egg

⅔ cup milk

2 tablespoons sugar

1 (8.5-ounce) box Jiffy Corn Muffin mix

½ cup Bisquick mix

Cook sausage, then cut each link into 4 pieces. Spray a mini muffin pan generously with cooking spray, then place 1 piece of sausage into muffin cups (may have to cook these in 2 batches).

Add egg, milk, and sugar to a medium bowl, and beat with a fork until combined. Add muffin mix and Bisquick, and stir until smooth. Spoon batter over sausage pieces until muffin cups are a little more than ¾ full. Bake at 400° for 10 minutes, or until golden brown. Remove from oven, and cool in pan for 10 minutes. Serve with syrup for dipping.

TO FREEZE:
Cool muffins completely; add to a zip-top freezer bag. Freeze for up to 3 months. Reheat in microwave or toaster oven until heated through.

Sausage and Cheese Grits Casserole

I came home on my birthday one year to find a copy of the annual Taste of Home 2012 Holiday & Celebrations cookbook. I flipped it open and didn't have to look far before I stumbled across a full-page feature of me and this recipe! Happy birthday to ME! Holla! That was a first!

2 pounds breakfast sausage

2 cups water

2 cups chicken broth

1 teaspoon salt

1¼ cups quick-cooking grits

1 pound shredded sharp Cheddar cheese

1 cup milk

6 tablespoons butter

1 teaspoon garlic powder

1 teaspoon paprika

1 teaspoon cayenne pepper (optional)

6 eggs, beaten

Brown sausage in a large skillet, stirring until it crumbles. Drain well, and set aside.

Bring water and chicken broth to a boil; stir in salt and grits then return to a boil. Cover pan, reduce heat to medium, and simmer 10 minutes, stirring occasionally. Remove from heat; add cheese, milk, butter, garlic, paprika, and cayenne pepper, stirring until cheese melts. Stir in sausage and eggs. Spoon mixture into a lightly greased 9x13-inch baking dish. Bake, uncovered, 350° for 45–55 minutes or until golden and bubbly and a knife inserted in the middle comes out clean. Let stand 15 minutes before serving.

Sausage and Cheese Grits Casserole

Creamy Cheese Grits

2 cups heavy cream

2 cups water or chicken stock

1 cup stone-ground grits

1 teaspoon salt

½ teaspoon coarse-ground black pepper

2 cups shredded Cheddar or Gruy re cheese

Heat cream and water or stock over medium heat until simmering. Add grits, salt, and pepper. Whisk grits until bubbly. Reduce heat to low, cover, and cook grits 1 hour, stirring occasionally.

Stir in cheese, and add more salt and/or pepper to taste, if necessary. Serve immediately.

Sausage Gravy

1 pound breakfast sausage

¼ cup all-purpose flour

2–3 cups milk

Salt and pepper to taste

Cook and crumble sausage in a large skillet until sausage is cooked through. Do not drain fat. Reduce heat to medium. Add flour to the skillet. Whisk the flour, sausage crumbles, and pan drippings together, and cook for 3–4 minutes, or until flour is light brown in color.

Reduce heat to medium low, then slowly add milk to pan, whisking constantly until smooth and well combined. Add salt and pepper to taste, and cook for 2–3 minutes. Add more milk, if needed, until desired consistency is reached. Serve immediately over biscuits or toast.

Bacon Gravy

Red eye gravy is the breakfast gravy I grew up eating. We had sausage gravy every now and again, mostly red eye, but NEVER bacon gravy! This is definitely a treat!

3 slices bacon, cooked, crumbled

2 tablespoons bacon grease

2 tablespoons all-purpose flour

1½ cups milk

Salt and pepper to taste

NOTE:
You may substitute vegetable oil for bacon grease, but any true southerner wouldn't consider it!

Once you've cooked your bacon, pour off all the grease, leaving all the glorious bits that cooked off in the pan.

Add 2 tablespoons of bacon grease back to the pan, and heat over medium-high heat. Add 2 tablespoons of flour to the hot oil. Whisk the flour and oil together, and cook for 3–4 minutes or until medium brown in color.

Reduce heat to medium-low then slowly add milk to pan, whisking constantly until smooth and well combined. Add crumbled bacon, salt, and pepper, and cook for 2–3 minutes. Add more milk, if needed, until desired consistency is reached. Serve immediately over biscuits or toast. Serves 4.

Tater Tot Breakfast Casserole

1 pound breakfast sausage

1 onion, chopped

1 green bell pepper, chopped

2 cups shredded Cheddar
cheese, divided

5 eggs

1½ cups milk

¾ teaspoon salt

¼ teaspoon granulated garlic

1 (32-ounce) package frozen
tater tots, thawed

Spray a 9x13-inch baking pan with cooking spray; set aside. Cook and crumble sausage, onion, and pepper in a large skillet until sausage is cooked through; drain fat. Spread sausage mixture into prepared pan; top with ½ of cheese; set aside.

Whisk together eggs, milk, salt, and garlic, then pour mixture over sausage and cheese. Arrange tater tots on top of casserole in a single layer. Bake, uncovered, for 35–40 minutes or until tater tots become golden brown. Remove from oven, and sprinkle remaining cheese evenly over tater tots. Return to oven until cheese is melted. Let stand 15 minutes before serving.

Soups, Stews & Chilis

This Ranch Chicken Chili is so AH-MAZE-ING. But you want to know what's the best thing about it? It's ridiculously easy.

Hamburger Vegetable Beef Soup

I loved this soup so much when I was a kid (they served it at school) that I set out to re-create it a few years ago and came up with this recipe.

1 pound lean ground beef (90/10 or better)

1 small onion, diced

Salt and pepper to taste

2 (16-ounce) cans mixed vegetables (such as Veg-All), undrained

1 (15-ounce) can petite diced tomatoes, undrained

1 can water

1 large potato, peeled and cubed

5 beef bouillon cubes (or equivalent amount of granules)

½ teaspoon Italian seasoning

¼ teaspoon dried thyme

Brown ground beef with onion, salt, and pepper in a soup pot until beef is cooked through. Do not drain. (GASP! Trust me, you need the fat and flavor, and we're using lean ground beef, remember?) Add remaining ingredients, and simmer over medium-low heat for 1 hour.

Remove from heat, and allow soup to rest for 30 minutes before serving.

Stuffed Pepper Soup

1½ pounds lean ground beef

1 large onion, chopped

1 large bell pepper, seeded and chopped

1 (28-ounce) can petite diced tomatoes

1 (10-ounce) can condensed tomato soup

1 (32-ounce) carton chicken broth

1 cup uncooked white rice

½ teaspoon pepper

½ teaspoon granulated garlic

¼ teaspoon dried basil

1 teaspoon salt

1 tablespoon sugar

Brown ground beef with onion and bell pepper in a large pot or Dutch oven until meat is cooked through. Do not drain fat. Add remaining ingredients, and bring to a boil. Once boiling, reduce heat to low, cover, and cook for 30 minutes or until rice is tender. Remove from heat and let rest, covered, for 15 minutes before serving.

Cajun Ham and Bean Soup

My family has been making this for years.

1 ham bone

1 package 15-Bean Soup Mix

8 cups water

1 teaspoon cayenne pepper

1 teaspoon granulated garlic

½–1 teaspoon salt, or to taste

½ teaspoon dried oregano

½ teaspoon dried thyme

½ teaspoon onion powder

½ teaspoon black pepper

1 bay leaf

2 cups chopped ham

Add all ingredients except ham to a large soup pot or Dutch oven. Bring to a boil, then reduce heat to medium low, cover, and simmer for 4 hours.

Remove ham bone. Trim away all the meat from the joint and bone, and add meat to the soup pot; give the bone to your dog. Add the additional 2 cups chopped ham, and stir well to incorporate. Cover, and continue cooking on low for 2–3 hours or until beans are tender.

Tastes great served over hot rice.

NOTE:

If you use Cajun variety soup mix, disregard other spices and seasonings in this recipe and go with the packet; salt to taste. If you can't find the Cajun variety, then you need to use all these spices.

Carolina She-Crab Soup

1 small onion, grated

1 stalk celery, grated

1 large carrot, grated

1 clove garlic, minced

¼ cup butter

¼ cup all-purpose flour

1 quart half-and-half

1 pint heavy cream

2 cups fish stock or chicken broth

¾ teaspoon salt

½ teaspoon white pepper

1 bay leaf

1 pound lump crabmeat

½ cup dry sherry, plus more for serving, if desired

Sauté onion, celery, carrot, and garlic in butter over medium heat until onions are translucent. Add flour, and continue cooking for 3–4 minutes or until butter is a light golden brown. Whisk in half-and-half, and stir until creamy. Add cream, fish stock (or chicken broth), salt, pepper, and bay leaf, and stir until smooth. Bring soup to a simmer, then reduce heat to medium-low, cover, and continue cooking for 30 minutes. For a thicker soup, simmer uncovered until soup is reduced to desired consistency. For a thinner soup, add milk.

Remove bay leaf then stir in crabmeat and sherry, cover, and continue cooking 5 minutes. Add more salt, if necessary. Remove from heat and let rest, covered, for 10 minutes before serving. Serve each bowl with a splash of sherry, if desired.

Broccoli Cheddar Soup

1 small onion, finely diced

1 large carrot, finely diced

2–3 cloves garlic, minced

6 tablespoons butter

¼ cup all-purpose flour

2 cups half-and-half

2 cups chicken broth

1 teaspoon salt

½ teaspoon pepper

4 cups chopped broccoli florets

**8 ounces Cheddar cheese,
shredded (about 2 cups)**

Sauté onion, carrot, and garlic in butter over medium heat until onions are translucent. Add flour, and continue cooking for 3–4 minutes or until butter is a light golden brown. Whisk in half-and-half, and stir until creamy. Add chicken broth, salt, and pepper, and stir until smooth. Bring soup to a simmer then reduce heat to medium-low, cover, and continue cooking for 15 minutes.

Add broccoli, and continue cooking for 10 minutes or until broccoli is tender. Add cheese, and stir until melted and creamy. Reduce heat to low until ready to serve.

Mama's Shellfish Chowder

1 cup diced celery

1 large onion, diced

½ cup butter

2 cloves garlic, minced

3 cups water

5–6 small/medium potatoes,
   peeled and diced into
   ½-inch cubes

1 tablespoon salt

½ teaspoon black pepper

2 bay leaves

½ pound scallops

1 pound shrimp, peeled

1 can clams (with juice)

1 pint half-and-half

½ cup dry white wine

Sauté celery and onion in butter in a large stock pot over medium heat 5 minutes. Add garlic, and continue cooking for 2 minutes. Add water, potatoes, salt, pepper, and bay leaves; cover, and simmer for 30 minutes. Add scallops and remaining ingredients, return to a simmer, and continue cooking for 5 minutes. Remove from heat, and allow to rest, covered, for 15–20 minutes before serving.

VARIATION:
You can add lump crabmeat as well for an extra special chowder.

Tuscan Chicken Stew

1 (5- to 6-pound) chicken

2 cups water

4 cups chicken broth

2–3 teaspoons salt, divided

1½ teaspoons black pepper, divided

1 bay leaf

4 stalks celery, diced

3 carrots, diced

1 large onion, diced

5 medium red potatoes, sliced

1 (15-ounce) can Great Northern beans, drained and rinsed

1 teaspoon dried thyme

6 cloves garlic, minced

½ teaspoon paprika

½ teaspoon red pepper flakes

½ teaspoon Italian seasoning

In a large Dutch oven or soup pot, add chicken, water, chicken broth, 1 teaspoon salt, 1 teaspoon black pepper, and bay leaf; boil, then cover and simmer over medium-low heat for 1 hour. Remove chicken, and set aside to cool. Pour broth through strainer, and add broth back to Dutch oven.

Bring broth to a boil, and add remaining ingredients, except tomatoes. Reduce heat to medium, and cook uncovered for 45 minutes.

Meanwhile, remove skin and bones from chicken; shred or chop chicken; cover and set aside.

Once vegetables and broth have cooked for 45 minutes, add chicken, and stir to combine. Cover pot, remove from heat, and let stew rest for 30 minutes. Stir, and serve with cornbread or crusty bread.

Husband's Favorite Beef Stew

Sitting at the supper table, my husband grabbed my hand, looked me square in the eye, and said, "This is the best thing you've ever cooked since the day I met you."

1 (3- to 4-pound) chuck roast

Salt and pepper to taste

3 tablespoons vegetable oil

2 cups chopped carrots

2 onions, chopped

2 envelopes beefy onion soup mix (such as Lipton's)

¾ teaspoon granulated garlic*

3 cups water

2 tablespoons Worcestershire

8–10 small potatoes, quartered

¼ cup cornstarch

*Garlic powder can be substituted for granulated garlic..

Cut chuck roast into 1½- to 2-inch pieces, and season with salt and pepper. Heat vegetable oil in a large skillet over medium-high heat, and sear chuck roast pieces in batches (don't overcrowd the pan, or the meat won't sear properly). When seared, place chuck roast pieces in a large slow cooker. Add carrots and onions to slow cooker. Combine soup mix, garlic, water, and Worcestershire, and stir until soup mix is dissolved. Add soup mixture and potatoes to slow cooker, and stir to incorporate. Cover, and cook on LOW for 8 hours.

One hour before the stew is done, ladle out about ½ cup of broth. Set aside to cool. Increase slow cooker temperature to HIGH. Whisk cornstarch into cooled broth until smooth, then stir into stew. Cover, and continue cooking for 30 minutes or until broth has thickened.

Sausage Steam Pot with Potatoes and Cabbage

1 head cabbage

2½ pounds small potatoes (I used Honey Gold)

2 pounds smoked sausage, sliced into 2-inch pieces

1 (14-ounce) can chicken broth

Salt and pepper to taste

Clean cabbage, and slice off the dirty party of the stump where the stem was. Cut the cabbage into 10–12 wedges. Don't remove the core, as it will keep the wedges together. Layer cabbage wedges, potatoes, and sausage pieces into a large pot; season each layer with salt and pepper. Pour chicken broth into pot. Bring pot to a boil, then cover tightly, and reduce heat to medium low. Cook 1–2 hours, or until potatoes are very tender.

If using a slow cooker, cook on LOW for 8–10 hours, or HIGH for 4–6 hours, until potatoes are very tender.

Potato Goulash with Sausage

However you like your goulash, you ought to give this one a try, because it sure is good! I made it and fell in love with it. I sopped up the rich potato-y, stew-y broth with a hunk of crusty bread, and came close to hurting myself when I went back for seconds.

2 tablespoons vegetable oil

2 medium yellow onions, halved lengthwise and then sliced

1 teaspoon paprika

1 teaspoon salt

½ teaspoon granulated garlic

½ teaspoon black pepper

6 small russet potatoes, peeled and sliced into ½-inch slices

1 (14½-ounce) can beef broth (about 1¾ cups)

1 pound smoked sausage, sliced thick, browned

Heat vegetable oil in 12-inch Dutch oven or heavy skillet. Add onions to hot oil, and sauté 5 minutes. Add paprika, salt, garlic, and pepper, and continue cooking 2 more minutes. Add potato slices to onions, and stir until potatoes are nicely coated with onions and seasonings.

Add beef broth, and bring to a slight boil. Reduce heat to medium. Continue simmering, uncovered, 15 minutes, stirring occasionally, checking to make sure potatoes stay submerged in the broth (add more broth if necessary).

Stir in sausage, reduce heat to low, and continue cooking, uncovered, until potatoes are tender, stirring occasionally.

NOTE:

It is important to use a pot close to 12 inches in diameter to ensure the broth will be deep enough to cook the potatoes.

Ranch Chicken Chili

This chili is so AH-MAZE-ING. But you want to know what's the best thing about it? It's ridiculously easy.

3 large chicken breasts

Salt, pepper, and granulated garlic to taste

2–3 tablespoons olive or vegetable oil

1 onion, diced

1 jalapeño pepper, seeded and diced (optional)

1 (1-ounce) packet ranch dressing mix

1 (1.25-ounce) packet taco seasoning

1 (16-ounce) can pinto beans

1 (15-ounce) can Great Northern beans

1 (4-ounce) can diced green chiles

Shredded cheese and/or chopped cilantro (optional)

Cut chicken into bite-sized pieces, and season with salt, pepper, and granulated garlic. Heat oil in a large pan or Dutch oven over medium-high heat. Add chicken, onion, and jalapeño, and sauté until chicken is browned (we're not trying to cook it through, just to sear it a little). Cook chicken in 2 batches, if necessary, so not to overcrowd the pan.

Add ranch dressing mix and taco seasoning. Add beans and chiles with liquid (do not drain or rinse), and stir until all ingredients are combined. Reduce heat to low, and cook for 1–4 hours.

Serve with shredded cheese and/or chopped cilantro, if desired.

SLOW COOKER PREPARATION:

Follow the instructions above, then add all ingredients to slow cooker, and cook on LOW for 6–8 hours, or HIGH for 3–4 hours. Serve with shredded cheese and/or chopped cilantro.

Ranch Chicken Chili

Easy Slow Cooker Chili

I know all the packets of chili seasoning have a recipe on the back, but this is the way I always, always make mine, and it turns out perfect every single time.

2–2½ pounds ground beef

1 onion, chopped

Salt and pepper to taste

2 (14-ounce) cans petite diced tomatoes

2 (8-ounce) cans tomato sauce

2 (16-ounce) cans pinto beans, drained

2 (1.75-ounce) packages chili seasoning mix

¾ teaspoon granulated garlic

½ teaspoon oregano

½ teaspoon red pepper flakes (optional)

1 (12-ounce) can beer (may sub vegetable stock or water)

Brown ground beef with onion, salt, and pepper over high heat. Drain fat then add ground beef to slow cooker. Add tomatoes, tomato sauce, beans, chili seasoning, garlic, oregano, red pepper flakes, and beer to ground beef, and stir until well combined. Cover and cook on high for 5–6 hours, or low for 8–10 hours. The beer makes the chili!

Salads

I usually make my chicken salad one of two ways; either super basic with just mayo, thyme, salt, and pepper, or super swanky with grapes or raisins and pecans. But I had this gorgeous, leafy bunch of celery, and it was talking to me. The next thing I knew I was thinking about chicken wings and voilà! I made this Buffalo Chicken Salad.

Easy Good Egg Salad

I'm a purist when it comes to egg salad (I'm the same way with deviled eggs). I don't like it sweet, and I don't like a lot of mustard.

12 large eggs

⅓ cup mayonnaise

½ teaspoon yellow mustard

Dash of salt

Cover eggs with cold water in a large pan, and bring to a boil. Once boiling, cover pan tightly with a lid, and remove from heat. Let eggs rest, covered, for 20 minutes.

Pour water off, and fill pan with ice and cold water. Let rest for 5 minutes, then peel eggs. Dice eggs, and place in a bowl.

In a small bowl, combine mayonnaise, mustard, and salt, and mix well. Add mayonnaise mixture to eggs, and stir until yolks are smooth. Add more mayonnaise, 1 tablespoon at a time, until desired consistency is reached. Taste for salt, and add more, if necessary. Add more mustard, if desired. If you like it sweet, substitute mayonnaise with salad dressing or add sweet pickle relish. Cover, and refrigerate until ready to serve.

Southern-Style Potato Salad

Now, this is a recipe that will likely start a riot. Just like with cornbread dressing, macaroni and cheese, and sweet potato casserole, every southerner has their own version. And if yours doesn't taste like ours, we probably won't like it. We're awesome like that!

6 medium russet potatoes, peeled and cut into 1-inch cubes

Salted water

6 boiled eggs, peeled and chopped

⅓ cup sweet pickle relish

1 cup mayonnaise

1 heaping tablespoon Dijon mustard

¾ teaspoon salt

¾ teaspoon black pepper

Boil potatoes in liberally salted water for 15–20 minutes, or until tender. Drain in colander, and rinse thoroughly. Add potatoes, eggs, and pickle relish to a mixing bowl; set aside. Combine mayonnaise, mustard, salt, and pepper in a small bowl, and whisk until thoroughly combined. Add mayonnaise mixture to potato mixture, and gently fold until all ingredients are thoroughly combined. I like mine on the "mashy" side, so I get a little rough with mine, but if you like a firmer texture, go easy. Refrigerate until ready to serve.

Picnic Pasta Salad

I call this Picnic Pasta Salad because this is what I like to bring to picnics, barbeques, or covered-dish events during the spring or summer. Since it doesn't have any mayonnaise or mayonnaise-based dressing, you don't have to stress too much over keeping it cold.

1 pound rotini pasta, uncooked

Salted water

2 medium cucumbers, peeled and chopped

1 pint grape tomatoes, halved

1 bunch green onions, chopped

1 (6-ounce) jar green olives, drained and halved

2 teaspoons minced garlic

1⅓ cups Kraft's Zesty Italian salad dressing

Cook pasta al dente per package instructions in liberally salted water. Drain pasta, and rinse in cold water until pasta is cool to the touch. Drain well. Combine pasta with remaining ingredients; stir to combine. Refrigerate until ready to serve.

VARIATIONS:

Italian: Omit cucumbers and green olives, and add: black olives and/or diced green bell peppers, mozzarella cubes, pepperoni slices, and Parmesan cheese.

Greek: Omit green onions, green olives, and Italian dressing, and add: Kalamata olives, red onion, crumbled feta, and Greek dressing.

Creamy Macaroni Salad

My mom put some of this in a container and gave it me to take home. I glanced at it and thought, meh. It sat in the fridge untouched, then after a few days, I brought it to work with me to eat for lunch, but really couldn't muster any enthusiasm to eat it. When my stomach started munching on my backbone, I finally grabbed it and decided to eat some. Oh. My. It was so good! I just assumed it was pasta, mayo, and a few minced veggies, so I was blown away at the flavor! Like, truly shocked!

1 pound small ridged elbow macaroni noodles or corkscrew pasta

Liberally salted water

2–3 tablespoons dried parsley

¼ teaspoon granulated garlic

¼ teaspoon salt

¼ teaspoon black pepper

1 tablespoon Dijon mustard

1⅓ cups mayonnaise

1 tablespoon white vinegar

1 red onion, finely diced

¾ cup finely diced celery

Cook pasta al dente per package instructions in liberally salted water. Drain pasta then rinse in cold water. Drain again, then immediately add pasta to a large mixing bowl, and mix with parsley, garlic, salt, pepper, and Dijon mustard, stirring until well combined. Let pasta "marinate" in the seasonings for 15–20 minutes, uncovered, at room temperature to allow the pasta to soak up the seasonings. Whip together mayonnaise and vinegar, and set aside.

Add onion, celery, and mayonnaise mixture to pasta, and stir until all ingredients are thoroughly combined. Cover, and refrigerate 1–4 hours. Before serving, mix well, then add more salt or mayo to taste, if desired.

NOTE:
Use any small, tubular, ridged pasta for this recipe. I think ridged pasta is best for pasta salads, because the ridges help the other ingredients stick to the pasta.

Ranch BLT Pasta Salad

I used my Creamy Macaroni Salad recipe as a jumping off point for this BLT salad, because it is such a great recipe.

½ pound small ridged elbow macaroni or corkscrew pasta

Salted water

1 tablespoon dried parsley

¼ teaspoon granulated garlic

¼ teaspoon salt

¼ teaspoon black pepper

2 teaspoons Dijon mustard

1 (12-ounce) package bacon (You can use less if you're using lean or center-cut bacon.)

1 head romaine lettuce

½ cup mayonnaise

¼ cup ranch dressing

1 teaspoon white vinegar

1 pint grape or cherry tomatoes, halved

5–6 green onions, chopped (optional)

VARIATION:
Add chopped chicken and/or chopped avocados.

Cook pasta al dente in liberally salted water per package instructions. Drain pasta then rinse in cold water. Drain again, then place pasta in a large mixing bowl. Don't let it sit and dry out too much; the pasta should be on the moist side.

Add parsley, garlic, salt, pepper, and Dijon mustard to pasta, and stir until well combined. Let pasta "marinate" in the seasonings for 15–20 minutes, uncovered, at room temperature. (This allows the pasta to soak up the flavors before adding the mayonnaise mixture.)

While pasta is "marinating," slice bacon into ½-inch ribbons, and cook until crispy; drain, and set aside.

Remove softer, outer leaves from lettuce. Roughly chop approximately 4 cups from the inner (more crunchy) leaves; set aside.

Whip together mayonnaise, ranch dressing, and vinegar, then add mixture to the cooked pasta, and stir to combine. Add half the bacon, tomato halves, chopped romaine, and green onions to pasta, and gently stir until all ingredients are thoroughly combined. Top with remaining half of bacon, and serve immediately.

If not serving this immediately, mix all but the romaine and second half of bacon. When you're ready to serve, toss pasta with romaine, then top with remaining half of the bacon.

Ranch BLT Pasta Salad

Husband-Approved Tuna Salad

Really? A recipe for tuna salad? Well, yes, really. For two reasons: 1) because my friends assure me that people do, indeed, actually need even the most basic recipes, and 2) because this the only way my husband likes tuna salad . . . and he feels pretty strongly about it.

1 (12-ounce) can chunk light tuna, very well drained

½ cup finely diced onion

½ teaspoon Old Bay Seasoning

Black pepper to taste

¼ cup mayonnaise

Combine all ingredients, and stir until thoroughly combined. Refrigerate until ready to serve.

NOTE:
If you don't have Old Bay, use ⅓ teaspoon of salt, and if you have it, a pinch of celery seed.

Leftover Ham Salad

Here's my recipe for Leftover Ham Salad . . . and I love it. Like? No, I love, love, love it. As in, get-up-at-midnight, go-downstairs, and eat-it-out-of-the-container-with-a-spoon, love it.

3½–4 cups chopped ham (pulse in the food processor only 3–5 times)

½ cup mayonnaise

⅓ cup sweet pickle relish

Combine all ingredients, and stir well. Add more mayo and/or relish to your liking. Serve as sandwich spread or with crackers. Store in refrigerator.

NOTE:
I've only made this using leftover baked ham, so I can't advise if this will taste as yummilicious or have the same perfectly perfect texture if you use some other type of ham (deli, canned, etc.).

Golden Pecan Chicken Salad

This is my fancy-schmancy chicken salad recipe. I've called this one Golden Pecan because it has golden raisins and pecans (which is my favorite combination), but when you look below, you'll see different fruit and nut options if mine aren't your favorite.

2 cups chopped, cooked chicken breasts

1 tablespoon olive oil

½ teaspoon dried thyme

½ teaspoon salt

½ cup mayonnaise

½ cup chopped pecans

½ cup golden raisins

NUT ALTERNATIVES:

½ cup slivered almonds

½ cup chopped walnuts

½ cup pistachios

⅓ cup sunflower seeds

FRUIT ALTERNATIVES:

½ cup dried cranberries

½ cup pineapple tidbits in heavy syrup, drained well

1 cup chopped apples

1 cup halved or quartered grapes

Combine chicken, olive oil, thyme, and salt in a medium bowl, and mix well. Cover, and refrigerate at least 30 minutes (or up to 4 hours). Add mayo, pecans, and raisins, and mix well. Salt to taste, if necessary. Cover, and refrigerate until ready to serve.

Classic Chicken Salad

There's a little trick to this recipe that you don't want to skip. I saw Julia Child do this once on a cooking show, and it's been scorched into my brain ever since. You "marinate" the cooked chicken in the seasonings and a little olive oil before adding the other ingredients. This helps the chicken absorb the flavors and stay moist. The end result is more flavorful, and you don't have to use as much mayo. Double score!

2 cups chopped, cooked chicken breasts

1 tablespoon olive oil

1 teaspoon dried thyme

½ teaspoon salt

½ teaspoon pepper

¼ cup mayonnaise

Combine chicken, olive oil, thyme, salt, and pepper in a medium bowl, and mix well. Cover, and refrigerate at least 30 minutes (or up to 4 hours). Add mayo, and mix well. Add more salt to taste, if necessary, and/or more mayo. Cover, and refrigerate until ready to serve.

VARIATION:
Feel free to add minced celery, diced onion, sweet pickle relish, chopped boiled eggs, or anything else to suit your fancy (you'll likely need more than ¼ cup of mayo if you add extra stuff, especially boiled eggs).

NOTE:
Any leftover chicken will work, but when I'm making this from scratch, I poach chicken breasts in a little water liberally seasoned with salt and pepper. And I always, always, always use the bone-in split chicken breasts with skin, because the chicken is so much more flavorful than boneless/skinless chicken breasts. And when I'm done, I have a rich, yummy chicken stock left over to pop in the freezer for later use.

Buffalo Chicken Salad

I usually make my chicken salad one of two ways; either super basic with just mayo, thyme, salt, and pepper, or super swanky with grapes or raisins and pecans. But I had this gorgeous, leafy bunch of celery, and it was talking to me. The next thing I knew I was thinking about chicken wings and voilà! . . . I made this Buffalo Chicken Salad.

⅓ **cup mayonnaise**

1 tablespoon hot sauce (such as Texas Pete)

Dash of garlic powder

2 large chicken breasts, cooked, chopped

1 stalk celery, finely chopped

Salt and pepper to taste

In a medium bowl, whisk together mayonnaise, hot sauce, and garlic. Add chopped chicken, celery, salt, and pepper, then mix well.

Serve with crackers and/or celery sticks. Consider serving with a wedge of bleu cheese or Brie.

Chicken Caesar Supper Salad

As I was shopping for the ingredients for a salad, I piled some hearts of romaine, Parmesan, and Caesar dressing in the shopping cart, and was feeling pretty good about how this was going to come together with my marinated chicken strips. Then I spied one of those family-size Caesar salad kits in the produce section and thought— even better! This was going to be the best salad supper. EVER! Voilà, y'all!

2 large (or 3 small) boneless, skinless chicken breasts

3 tablespoons olive oil

1 tablespoon oregano

1 teaspoon granulated garlic

½ teaspoon salt

½ teaspoon pepper

1 family-size Caesar salad kit (or 2 small ones)

Do this ahead to have ready for your salad. Cut chicken breasts into thin strips (about ½ inch wide). Add chicken, olive oil, oregano, garlic, salt, and pepper to a zip-top bag. Seal bag, and "massage" the chicken around a bit to evenly distribute the seasonings. Marinate chicken in the refrigerator 6–10 hours.

When ready to assemble, heat a large skillet over medium-high heat. Add half of chicken strips to hot skillet, and sauté until lightly browned; set aside. Cook the remaining chicken; set aside. Assemble salad per package instructions, and place on serving plates. Top salad with chicken, and serve.

NOTE:
I was able to make 2 adult and 2 child-sized salads from this recipe. Adjust recipe for your family, as needed.

Southern-Style Coleslaw

Mama and I are a lot alike in many ways. One thing we have in common is that we always forget the coleslaw (and deviled eggs) in the fridge when it's time to eat. Now, I know there are lots of cool coleslaw mixes out there, and you can buy the pre-shredded cabbage nowadays, but if you want real-deal southern-style coleslaw, you've got to shred your own cabbage.

1 head cabbage, finely shredded

1 carrot, finely shredded

½ cup mayonnaise

⅓ cup granulated sugar

⅓ cup milk

3 tablespoons white vinegar

2 teaspoons grated horseradish (or to taste)

¾ teaspoon salt

½ teaspoon pepper

Add shredded cabbage and carrot to a large mixing bowl; set aside. In a smaller bowl, combine remaining ingredients, and mix well. Add mayonnaise mixture to cabbage and carrots, and mix well. Cover tightly, and refrigerate until ready to serve.

Homemade Croutons

We eat a big fat salad at least once a week for supper. Sometimes I like to make fresh, hot, chewy, crusty croutons to go with our salad. They're sooooo good and sooooo easy and sooooo much better than store-bought croutons.

Here's what you do . . . any time you have leftover buns or rolls (usually hamburger and hot dog buns at my house), just throw them in the freezer. They are perfect for croutons! And since I almost always buy whole-wheat buns, we get to have whole-wheat croutons—holla! Also, frozen buns are super easy to cut into crisp little cubes.

4 cups cubed leftover bread, rolls, or buns

¼ teaspoon salt

½ teaspoon garlic powder

1 teaspoon Italian seasoning (or parsley, or whatever seasoning you like)

3 tablespoons butter, melted

Add bread cubes to a large bowl, then add salt, garlic powder, and Italian seasoning; toss to evenly distribute seasoning throughout bread cubes. Drizzle melted butter over bread cubes, and toss to coat (I use my hands). Arrange bread cubes on a large baking sheet, and bake at 375° for 12–15 minutes.

NOTE:
I like mine crusty on the outside but kinda chewy on the inside, so I don't cook mine as long as some might prefer. Just take a look and take a taste, and cook them until you get them how you like them (how's that for a scientific recipe?).

Always Welcome Watergate Salad

1 (20-ounce) can crushed
   pineapple with juice

1 (3.4-ounce) package
   pistachio instant pudding
   mix

1 cup miniature marshmallows

½ cup chopped pecans

1 (8-ounce) tub frozen whipped
   topping, thawed

Combine first 4 ingredients, and mix well. Gently fold in whipped topping. Refrigerate until ready to serve.

Awesome Ambrosia Salad

1 (11-ounce) can mandarin
   oranges, drained

1 (5-ounce) jar maraschino
   cherries, drained

1 (20-ounce) can pineapple
   chunks, drained

1 cup sweetened flaked coconut

1 cup sour cream

1 cup mini marshmallows

1 cup chopped pecans

Mix all ingredients together, cover, and refrigerate 4–6 hours. Stir before serving.

Holiday Cranberry Salad

Guess what my friend, Dawn, brought to our Thanksgiving dinner? Cranberry sauce. And guess what else . . . I don't like cranberry sauce! Or anything that resembles it. And I didn't want any of it near my turkey on Thanksgiving. But, to be polite, I put about ⅛ of a teaspoon on my plate. And then everyone at the table started raving about it. So I tasted it. EAU MAH GAH, y'all. It was SO GOOD!

1 (3-ounce) box raspberry gelatin

1 cup boiling water

¾ cup sugar

1 tablespoon lemon juice

1 (8-ounce) can crushed pineapple, with juice

3–4 cups frozen cranberries

½ cup finely chopped walnuts

½ cup finely diced celery

Dissolve gelatin in boiling water in a medium bowl; add sugar and lemon juice, and stir until sugar is dissolved. Add pineapple with juice. Chop frozen cranberries until uniform in size with the chopped walnuts and celery (cranberries must be frozen to chop properly). Process or chop enough cranberries to measure 2 cups. Add chopped cranberries, walnuts, and celery to mixture, and stir to combine. Pour into a gelatin mold or glass serving dish. Cover, and refrigerate several hours, or until set.

Vegetables

So, if you didn't know this already, we southerners are pretty set in our ways when it comes to cooking certain dishes. Oh, we'll eat it your way and be polite about it. And cooking greens is no exception. We all do it differently. I've seen more than one southern food "expert" on television cook them in ways that made me grasp my chest and lean up against the door frame for a minute. This is how I was raised to cook Southern-Style Collard Greens.

Southern-Style Black-Eyed Peas

Something amazing happened this weekend, y'all! My Canadian, meat-and-potatoes husband ate black-eyed peas! And he LIKED them!

1 pound dried black-eyed peas

Water

1 medium onion, finely diced

¼ cup butter

2 smoked ham hocks

1 teaspoon salt, or more to taste

1 teaspoon black pepper

Soak peas in 6 cups water overnight (10–12 hours). Drain peas, rinse well with cold water, and then drain again. Set aside.

In a large stock pot or Dutch oven, sauté onion in butter until onion is translucent and tender. Add 4 cups water, ham hocks, 1 teaspoon salt, pepper, and drained peas to pot. Cover, and simmer over medium-low heat for 4 hours, stirring occasionally.

Remove ham hocks, and trim off ham, discarding bones, cartilage, and skin. Add ham pieces back to peas, and stir. Add more salt to taste then simmer peas on low for 1 additional hour. If you have more liquid than you'd like, simmer on medium heat, uncovered, until liquid has reduced to your liking.

I usually serve mine over white rice with some fresh diced onion sprinkled on top, but you can serve them on their own as well. Really good with Skillet Cornbread (see page 40), too.

NOTE:

Use ham hocks, a leftover ham bone, or even a smoked turkey leg. If you can't find or don't have any of these, season with several drops of liquid smoke.

Cowboy Beans

I LOVE this recipe! I usually make it for a big weekend meal like a cookout or Sunday dinner, and then have enough leftovers to serve again during the week as a side dish.

1 pound ground beef

1 onion, diced

Salt and pepper to taste

2 (28-ounce) cans basic, plain-jane pork n' beans

¼ teaspoon chili powder

½ teaspoon granulated garlic

½ cup barbeque sauce

½ cup ketchup

½ cup brown sugar

Brown ground beef and onion with salt and pepper to taste until meat is cooked through. Drain fat then add meat mixture to a slow cooker or large saucepan.

Open cans of beans, and pour off any liquid that's settled at the top. Add beans and remaining ingredients to the meat mixture, and stir to incorporate. For slow cooker cooking, cook on LOW for 4–6 hours. For stove-top cooking, heat over medium-high heat until simmering, then reduce heat to low, and cook, covered, for 1 hour.

Squash Casserole

I've mentioned this before but . . . I don't really like casseroles. I'm sorry if we can't be friends now. It's the cream-of-whatever soups that throw me off. They're just so . . . processed tasting. Since casseroles are always chocked full of cheese and creamed soup and fried onions and tater tots and gummy bears and packing peanuts, they taste nothing like the star ingredient.

I'm not even sure that this recipe is an exception to the above, because I can't actually tell you it tastes all that much like squash. But I like it. A lot! Even though it has cream of whatever soup in it. It's like chicken and dressing and gravy all mixed up together with some squash hidden in it.

3 pounds yellow squash, washed and sliced

Salt and pepper to taste

1 medium onion, grated

1 large carrot, grated

1 can cream of chicken soup

1 cup sour cream

¼ cup butter, melted

3 cups Pepperidge Farm Herb Seasoned Stuffing

Boil squash in a little water with salt and pepper until tender; drain well, and add to a large bowl. Add onion, carrot, cream of chicken soup, sour cream, and butter, and mix well. Fold in 2 cups of the stuffing. Add mixture to a baking dish then top with remaining stuffing. Bake at 350° for 30–40 minutes or until golden brown and bubbly.

Crescent Roll Zucchini Pie

This recipe is a staple for my family. I'm still using the hand-written copy I scribbled down almost twenty years ago.

4–5 cups thinly sliced zucchini

1 large onion, diced

2 tablespoons butter

2 tablespoons dried parsley flakes

½ teaspoon salt

½ teaspoon pepper

½ teaspoon garlic powder

½ teaspoon dried oregano leaves

¼ teaspoon dried basil leaves

2 eggs, well beaten

2 cups shredded mozzarella cheese

2 teaspoons yellow mustard

1 (8-ounce) can crescent rolls

In a large skillet, sauté zucchini and onion in butter for 6–8 minutes or until tender. If your zucchini puts off more than ¼ cup of liquid, pour off excess. Stir in parsley flakes, salt, pepper, garlic powder, oregano, and basil. Remove from heat, and add eggs, cheese, and mustard; stir gently to mix.

Separate dough into 8 triangles. Place in ungreased 10-inch pie plate; press over bottom and up side to form crust. Firmly press perforations to seal. Pour zucchini mixture evenly into crust-lined pie plate. Bake at 350° for 25–30 minutes or until mostly set. If necessary, cover edge of crust with strips of foil during last 10 minutes of baking to prevent excessive browning. Remove from oven, and let stand, uncovered, for 15 minutes for pie to set up completely before serving.

Southern-Style Collard Greens

So, if you didn't know this already, we southerners are pretty set in our ways when it comes to cooking certain dishes. Oh, we'll eat it your way and be polite about it. And cooking greens is no exception. We all do it differently. I've seen more than one southern food "expert" on television cook them in ways that made me grasp my chest and lean up against the door frame for a minute. This is how I was raised to cook them.

1–2 bunches fresh collard greens

5 strips bacon, cut into ½-inch pieces

3 tablespoons additional bacon grease

1 onion, diced

Salt to taste

NOTE:
You may substitute vegetable or olive oil for bacon drippings, if necessary, but any southern cook will tell you that is simply not done!

Tear each leaf off the stalk, discarding the stalk. Plunge the leaves several times a clean sink full of cold water. Drain the sink, and rinse well. Trim the center rib (midrib) from each leaf, cutting each leaf into 2 halves, discarding the rib. Immerse leaves in cold water again. Drain.

Place 6–8 leaves in a stack, and roll tightly (like you're rolling a cigar). Slice roll into 1½-inch ribbons. Continue the process with remaining collards then set aside until ready to cook.

Using the biggest skillet or widest pot you have (that has a lid), cook bacon and bacon grease over medium-high heat, uncovered, until bacon is almost crisp. Add onions, and continue cooking until onions are translucent and bacon is crisp. Add as many collards as will fit in the skillet, and toss to coat in the bacon drippings. Cover skillet with lid, and let collards cook down (wilt) for 2–3 minutes. Add more collards, and repeat this step until all collards are in the skillet.

Reduce heat to low, salt to taste, and continue cooking, covered, for about an hour, or until collards are tender; stir occasionally. If your collards don't put off enough pot liquor (rendered liquid), add chicken stock or water, ¼ cup at a time, to ensure there's a little liquid (maybe a ¼ inch) in the bottom of the skillet at all times.

Southern-Style Collard Greens

Sweet Potato Praline Casserole

Around the holidays, this dish always makes its way to the table as a favorite among family and friends.

4 pounds sweet potatoes

¾–1 cup sugar (to taste)

1 teaspoon vanilla

½ teaspoon salt

2 eggs, beaten

6 tablespoons butter, melted

½ cup all-purpose flour

1 cup brown sugar

1 heaping cup chopped pecans

½ cup butter, melted

Pinch of salt

Arrange sweet potatoes on a baking sheet lined with aluminum foil, then pierce each with a fork a few times to vent. Bake at 400° until tender, about an hour. Check tenderness by inserting a knife into the thickest potato—knife should slide in easily with no resistance. Do not boil the potatoes or use canned ones. I mean it!

Allow sweet potatoes to cool to room temperature, then remove the skins. Add sweet potatoes, sugar, vanilla, salt, eggs, and butter to a medium bowl. Mix on medium speed with an electric mixer for 2 minutes, or until fluffy. Spoon sweet potato mixture evenly into a 9x9-inch casserole dish.

Combine flour, brown sugar, pecans, butter, and salt in a small bowl, and mix until crumbly . Mixture will be crumbly. Sprinkle topping evenly over sweet potato mixture. Bake at 350° for 30–35 minutes.

Baked Onion Rings

Since we were having the ultimate in junk food for supper one night, I wanted to serve a healthier alternative to the chips I was seriously considering. So I tried my hand at baking onion rings. They turned out delicious!

2–3 large onions, sliced into rings

¼ cup cornstarch

1½ cups Italian seasoned bread crumbs or panko

½ teaspoon salt

1 egg

3 tablespoons hot sauce

2 tablespoons milk

Separate onion slices into individual rings. Add cornstarch to a small bowl; set aside. Mix bread crumbs with salt in a small bowl; set aside. Whisk together egg, hot sauce, and milk in a small bowl until thoroughly combined; set aside.

Spray 2 cookie sheets with cooking spray. Dredge each onion ring first in the cornstarch, then egg wash, then bread crumbs. Place in a single layer on cookie sheets. Spray onion rings lightly with additional cooking spray (helps them crisp up a bit), and bake at 400° for 20 minutes or until golden brown, flipping after 10 minutes.

Hash Brown Casserole

2 (16-ounce) containers sour cream

2 packages ranch dressing mix (not dip)

3 cups shredded Cheddar cheese

1 (30-ounce) bag frozen shredded hash browns

¼ cup butter

Combine sour cream and ranch dressing mix in a large bowl. Add Cheddar cheese and hash browns, and stir to combine. Spray a 9x13-inch baking dish with cooking spray, then add hash brown mixture. Top mixture with pats of butter. Bake at 400° for 45–55 minutes or until golden brown and bubbly.

Loaded Smashed Potatoes

8 medium Yukon gold potatoes

8 slices bacon, diced

3 cloves garlic, minced

Salt and pepper to taste

½ cup sour cream

½ cup butter, at room temperature

2 cups shredded Cheddar cheese

½ cup chopped chives

ALTERNATIVE CASSEROLE PREPARATION:

Add ¼ cup milk to potatoes when adding sour cream. Spoon mixture into a small casserole dish, and top with 1½ cups shredded cheese (I think Monterey Jack would be AH-MAZE-ING). Bake at 375° for 25–30 minutes or until cheese is bubbly and slightly browned.

Wash unpeeled potatoes, and cut into large cubes (about 6 cubes for a medium potato). Boil in liberally salted water 15 minutes, or until tender. Drain potatoes; add to a large mixing bowl.

Meanwhile, sauté bacon over medium heat until slightly browned. Add garlic, and continue cooking for 2 minutes. Add crumbled bacon, garlic, and pan drippings to potatoes. Add salt, pepper, sour cream, butter, Cheddar cheese, and chives (reserving some chives for garnish, if desired); stir and mash with a large sturdy spoon until all ingredients are thoroughly incorporated and potatoes have reached your desired consistency. If you use a starchier potato, you might have to add a tad of milk at this point (if the dish seems too dry). Spoon potatoes into a medium-size dish, and serve.

Flat, Broke, and Busted Potatoes

I came across this recipe years ago and fell in love. We make them using whichever herbs we have on hand. Mom has enough fresh chives to sod the White House lawn, so that's what we used when we cooked this batch.

10–12 red potatoes (or however many you'd like to serve)

Salted water

Olive oil

2–3 teaspoons minced garlic

Coarse grain salt

Black pepper

Chopped fresh chives

Sour cream (optional)

Boil potatoes in liberally salted water until fork-tender, about 15 minutes. Drain potatoes, and place on a large baking sheet. Using the heel of your hand, a potato masher, or whatever gets the job done, press down on the potatoes until they're flat, broke, and busted. Drizzle each potato with olive oil. Top each potato with minced garlic, then sprinkle with salt, pepper, and chives.

Bake at 425° for 30–35 minutes, or until potatoes are golden brown and crispy around the edges. Serve with a dollop of sour cream, if desired.

Easy Lipton Onion Oven-Roasted Potatoes

I'd forgotten how simple and delicious these potatoes are! This recipe has been around for eons. You know why? Because it's GOOD.

6–8 medium potatoes

2 envelopes Lipton Onion Soup Mix

3–4 tablespoons olive oil

Black pepper and granulated garlic to taste

Sour cream and chopped chives (optional)

Ketchup (optional)

Wash potatoes, and cut into 1-inch pieces, leaving the skin on. Add potatoes, soup mixes, and olive oil to a large bowl, and toss to coat. Spray a large baking sheet with cooking spray then arrange potatoes in a single layer. (Use 2 pans if you have to—don't crowd these or layer them.) Top potatoes with any oil/soup mix left in the bowl. Once arranged on the baking sheet, season potatoes with pepper and garlic to taste. Bake at 425° for 35–45 minutes or until golden brown and crispy, flipping once with a sturdy spatula halfway through cooking. (I say use a sturdy spatula because the potatoes may stick to the bottom of the pan, and you'll need to scrape them off so the potatoes and skins stay intact.) Serve with sour cream and chives, or good ol' ketchup.

Easy Lipton Onion Oven-Roasted Potatoes

Southern-Style Baked Macaroni and Cheese

Down South, we don't serve this as a main course, only as a side dish, along with 6 other sides if it's Sunday! We're pretty serious about side dishes, y'all!

8 ounces uncooked extra large elbow macaroni (or ziti)

1 egg, beaten

1 cup sour cream

⅓ cup whole or evaporated milk

¼ cup butter, at room temperature

¾ teaspoon salt

½ teaspoon pepper

¼ teaspoon cayenne pepper

3 cups (12 ounces) shredded Cheddar cheese, divided

¼ teaspoon garlic salt

Cook pasta al dente in liberally salted water per package instructions. Drain pasta, and set aside. Whisk egg, sour cream, milk, butter, salt, pepper, and cayenne in a large bowl until well combined. Add pasta and 2 cups cheese, then toss to coat. Add mixture to a lightly buttered 1½-quart baking dish. Top with remaining 1 cup cheese. Sprinkle with garlic salt. Bake uncovered at 350° until browned and bubbly (35–40 minutes).

Baked Spaghetti

I think this is a cross between spaghetti and lasagna. A spaghagna. Or spasagna. Or whatever. Let's just call it baked spaghetti, because that's easier to say and doesn't make my head hurt.

1 pound ground beef

1 small onion, diced

Salt and pepper to taste

1 (24-ounce) jar prepared spaghetti sauce

1 cup ricotta cheese

1 egg, beaten

2 tablespoons milk

⅓ cup grated Parmesan cheese

½ teaspoon salt

½ teaspoon granulated garlic

½ teaspoon oregano or Italian seasoning blend

8 ounces uncooked spaghetti noodles, broken in half

8 ounces shredded mozzarella cheese (about 2 cups)

Cook pasta al dente in liberally salted water per package instructions. Drain pasta well; set aside. Meanwhile, cook ground beef with onion in a large skillet over medium-high heat until meat is cooked through, seasoning with salt and pepper to taste. Drain, then stir in spaghetti sauce; set aside. Combine ricotta cheese, egg, milk, Parmesan, salt, garlic, and oregano in a large bowl, and stir well; set aside. Add pasta to ricotta mixture; stir to combine. Spray a 9x13-inch baking dish with cooking spray, then spread pasta mixture evenly over bottom. Top evenly with meat mixture. Top meat mixture evenly with mozzarella cheese. Bake, uncovered, for 30–45 minutes at 350° or until bubbly and cheese starts to brown.

Everybody Loves Lasagna

1½ pounds ground beef

1 medium onion, diced

Salt and pepper to taste

1 (24-ounce) jar traditional spaghetti sauce

¼ teaspoon crushed red pepper

2 cups cottage or ricotta cheese

¾ cup grated Parmesan cheese, divided

1 egg, beaten

¼ cup chopped fresh parsley, plus more for garnish

½ teaspoon dried oregano

½ teaspoon granulated garlic

½ teaspoon salt

1 (16-ounce) block mozzarella cheese, divided

9–12 lasagna noodles

2 teaspoons olive oil

Brown ground beef with onion, salt, and pepper in a large skillet until meat is cooked through; drain fat from meat. Add spaghetti sauce and pepper; stir to combine. Reduce heat to low, cover, and simmer for 30 minutes.

Combine cottage or ricotta cheese, ½ cup Parmesan, egg, parsley, oregano, garlic, and salt; stir to combine; set aside. Divide mozzarella cheese in half. Shred one half, and slice the other half into thin slices. (If you don't have something to easily cut thin slices with, just shred all of your mozzarella.)

Cook pasta al dente in liberally salted water per package instructions. Drizzle the bottom of a large rectangular baking pan with olive oil. Arrange 3–4 noodles in a single layer in baking pan. Spread ⅓ of the cottage cheese mixture over noodles. Top cheese mixture with ⅓ meat sauce. Top meat sauce with ¼ of the mozzarella. Repeat these layers 2 times, adding remaining mozzarella and remaining ¼ cup Parmesan cheese to the top.

Cover dish with aluminum foil, and bake at 350° for 35–40 minutes or until bubbly. Remove aluminum foil from dish, and continue baking for 15–20 minutes or until cheese is nicely browned. Remove from oven, and let stand 15–20 minutes before serving. Garnish with fresh chopped parsley, if desired.

Everybody Loves Lasagna

Blackened Chicken Pasta Alfredo

2 tablespoons olive oil

3 large boneless, skinless chicken breasts

2 tablespoons Chicken Scratch (see page 112), divided

1 (15-ounce) jar prepared Alfredo sauce

¼ cup whole milk

10 ounces bow-tie pasta, cooked al dente, drained

Chopped fresh parsley for garnish

Heat olive oil in a large skillet over medium-high heat. Coat chicken with 1 tablespoon Chicken Scratch. Place in hot pan, and sear on each side until deeply browned. Cover pan with a tight-fitting lid, and remove from heat (chicken will finish cooking through so long as you leave it covered).

Pour Alfredo sauce in a medium-size pan, and heat on medium low. Add milk to sauce jar, and microwave on HIGH (without the lid) for 30 seconds. Replace lid, and shake vigorously. Add milk to pan. Add remaining 2 tablespoons Chicken Scratch, and stir well.

Slice chicken into strips. Combine pasta, sauce, and chicken, and toss to coat. Garnish with parsley, if desired.

Lemon Garlic Chicken

8 tablespoons salted butter

1 tablespoon minced garlic

1 pound chicken tenderloins

Salt to taste

2 tablespoons lemon juice

1 tablespoon parsley

4–6 cups egg noodles, cooked

3 tablespoons grated Parmesan cheese

Preheat oven 400°. Add butter to a 9x13-inch baking dish, and place in the oven to melt. Stir garlic into melted butter. Add chicken, toss to coat in butter mixture, then arrange in a single layer. Season chicken with salt, then bake for 15 minutes. Remove pan from oven. Baste chicken with garlic butter then drizzle with lemon juice, and sprinkle with parsley. Return to oven, and continue baking for 10 minutes. Remove chicken from pan, and set aside. Add cooked egg noodles and Parmesan to pan, and toss to coat in garlic butter; serve with chicken.

Italian Sausage Skillet Dinner

Just so you know . . . my husband said this was a "keeper," and to put it in the weekly line-up.

1 pound Italian sausage, casings removed

2 cloves garlic, minced

1 (24-ounce) jar chunky spaghetti sauce

2 cups water

1 teaspoon Italian seasoning

½ teaspoon salt

¼ teaspoon black pepper

8 ounces (2 cups) uncooked radiatore pasta (small ruffles)

¼ cup grated Parmesan cheese

Brown sausage in a 12-inch skillet over medium-high heat until cooked through. Add garlic, and continue cooking for 2 minutes. Add spaghetti sauce, water, Italian seasoning, salt, and pepper, and stir to combine. Add pasta, and cook until sauce starts to boil. Reduce heat to medium low, cover skillet, and continue cooking for 12 minutes, stirring occasionally. Remove skillet from heat, stir in Parmesan cheese, and let stand uncovered for 5–10 minutes, or until sauce has thickened. Stir once more before serving.

NOTE:
If you don't use a chunky sauce, you may need to reduce the water by 3–4 tablespoons.

Chicken Pilau

Chicken Pilau

1 large chicken

3½ cups water

2 stalks celery

3 teaspoons salt, divided

1 teaspoon black pepper

1 teaspoon onion powder

¾ teaspoon paprika

¾ teaspoon red pepper flakes

1 bay leaf

2 cups uncooked long-grain rice

1 pound smoked sausage

NOTE:
Be sure to use a liquid measuring cup, as dry and liquid measuring cups are not the same.

Clean chicken and rinse well; remove giblets, if included. Place chicken in Dutch oven (or large pot with a tight-fitting lid). Add water, celery, 2 teaspoons salt, and next 5 ingredients. Bring to a slow boil over medium heat. Once boiling, reduce heat to medium low, cover tightly, and simmer 1 hour. Remove chicken from broth, and set aside. Strain broth, and measure 4 cups liquid (not rendered fat— the fat will set on top of the broth). Set broth aside.

Remove skin, bones, etc. from chicken. Cut chicken into bite-sized pieces, and set aside. Slice sausage on a bias into bite-sized pieces. Add sausage, 4 cups broth, chicken pieces, remaining salt (I know this seems like a lot of salt, but there is a lot of rice here . . . just trust me), and uncooked rice to Dutch oven. Bring to a boil; reduce heat to medium low, and cover tightly. Cook for 20 minutes, stirring occasionally. Remove from heat, and let sit 20 minutes before serving.

Chicken and Sausage Dirty Rice

I love me some Dirty Rice. Especially the kind they have at Bojangle's. If you don't have a Bojangle's Famous Chicken and Biscuits where you live, you need to get in the car and drive South until you find one. Like, right now!

1 whole chicken

3½ cups water

2 teaspoons salt

1 teaspoon black pepper

1 teaspoon red pepper flakes

1 pound pork sausage

¾ cup finely diced celery

1 onion, diced

½ cup red or green bell pepper, finely diced (optional)

4–5 cloves garlic, minced

3 tablespoons dried parsley, or ½ cup chopped fresh parsley

2 teaspoons Cajun or Creole seasoning

2 cups uncooked long-grain rice

Clean chicken and rinse well; remove giblets, if included. Place chicken in Dutch oven (or large pot with a tight-fitting lid). Add water, salt, black pepper, and red pepper. Bring to a slow boil over medium heat. Once boiling, reduce heat to medium low, cover tightly, and simmer for 1 hour.

Remove chicken from broth, and set aside. Strain broth, and measure 4 cups liquid (not rendered fat—the fat will set on top of the broth). Set broth aside.

Remove skin, bones, etc. from chicken. Cut chicken into bite-sized pieces, and set aside. Sauté sausage, celery, onion, and bell pepper until sausage is cooked through. Add garlic and parsley, and stir to combine. Combine 4 cups broth, chicken pieces, sausage mixture, Cajun seasoning, and rice in your Dutch oven (or large pot with a tight-fitting lid). Bring to a boil; cover then reduce heat to medium low. Cook for 20 minutes, stirring occasionally.

Remove from heat, and let sit for 15 minutes or so before serving.

Broccoli Cheddar Chicken Casserole

For me to not care too much for cream-of-whatever soups, this Cheddar soup was surprisingly delicious!

1 cup milk

2 (10¾-ounce) cans Cheddar cheese soup (such as Campbell's)

1 teaspoon salt

1 cup white, long-grain rice, uncooked

3 large (or 4 small) boneless, skinless chicken breasts

Salt, pepper, and granulated garlic

1 (12-ounce) bag frozen broccoli florets, thawed (or about 3 cups fresh)

2 sleeves butter crackers, crushed (such as Ritz or Town House)

6 tablespoons butter, melted

¼ teaspoon granulated garlic

Spray the bottom and side of a 9x13-inch baking dish with cooking spray (or rub with butter); set aside. In a large bowl, whisk together milk, Cheddar soups, and 1 teaspoon salt until smooth. Set aside ⅓ of the soup mixture. To the remaining ⅔, fold in uncooked rice, and then pour mixture into prepared baking dish.

Cut chicken breasts into 1-inch pieces; sprinkle with salt, pepper, and granulated garlic. Arrange chicken pieces on top of rice mixture. Roughly chop broccoli florets, and arrange on top of the chicken. Pour reserved ⅓ of soup mixture evenly over broccoli. Cover dish tightly with aluminum foil, and bake at 350° for 45 minutes. Remove from oven, remove aluminum foil, and gently stir mixture until rice is evenly distributed throughout. Cover again, and continue baking for 15 more minutes.

Combine crushed crackers, melted butter, and granulated garlic, and mix well. Remove casserole from oven, remove aluminum foil, and then sprinkle cracker topping evenly over casserole. Continue baking, uncovered, for 15 minutes or until crackers start to brown. Remove from oven, and let rest for 10 minutes before serving.

NOTE:
May prepare ahead of time and refrigerate before cooking; you will either need to let it come to room temperature before cooking, or cook for an additional 10–15 minutes.

Stewed Beef and Rice

3 tablespoons vegetable oil

1½ pounds beef stew meat

Salt and pepper to taste

1 (14-ounce) can beef broth

1 envelope onion soup mix

1 cup water, divided

2 tablespoons cornstarch

Cooked rice

Heat oil in a large skillet over medium-high heat. Season stew meat with salt and pepper, then add to skillet, stirring to sear as many sides of meat as possible, for 3–4 minutes. Remove from heat; set aside.

In a medium-size stock pot, combine beef broth, onion soup mix, and ½ cup water; stir well. Add stew meat, stir, and cook over low heat, covered, for 1–2 hours. Do not let the pot reach a full, rolling boil, or the meat will get tough.

Remove stew meat with a slotted spoon; and set aside. Increase temperature of broth to medium-high, and bring to a boil. Add cornstarch to a small bowl, and whisk in remaining ½ cup of water until smooth. Drizzle cornstarch liquid into broth, return to a boil, and cook, while stirring, for 1 minute. Reduce heat to low. Once liquid has stopped boiling and has thickened, add stew meat back to pot, and stir to combine. (Don't leave the meat in the broth while boiling to thicken the cornstarch or—you guessed it—the meat will get tough.) Allow meat to get happy in the gravy for about 5 minutes, then serve over white rice.

NOTE:

The gravy finishes a little on the salty side, which is exactly how it should be when served with white rice. This isn't a stew; it's meant to be served over some sort of starch, so I make it saltier than I would an actual stew that's meant to be eaten on its own.

Greasy Rice

The most common question I get asked on my Facebook page is some variation of, "What the BLEEP is Greasy Rice?" Greasy rice is just plain white rice that is cooked in the stock and drippings rendered from slow cooking meat (usually pork or chicken).

2 cups pan juices from any slow-cooked meat

1 cup uncooked, long-grain white rice

Salt to taste

NOTE:

You can also substitute purchased broth or stock, but you'll need to add ¼–⅓ cup butter or bacon grease. If I've cooked meat that is especially fatty (a Boston butt, a pan of chicken thighs, etc.), I will often ladle off some of the fat. I've never measured how much fat I actually include, but if I had to guess, I'd say I like to have about ⅓ cup.

Using a 4-cup measuring pitcher, measure 2 cups of broth. The fat will settle on the top of the broth—do not consider the fat when measuring the broth. You need 2 full cups of liquid. If the meat you've cooked doesn't render a full 2 cups of liquid, add chicken broth or water until you have 2 full cups.

Add the broth (with fat) to a medium saucepan. Salt to taste. Add uncooked rice, and heat on high until boiling. Once boiling, cover, and reduce heat to medium low. Cook for 20 minutes, stirring occasionally. Remove from heat and let sit, covered, for 10 minutes. Fluff rice with a fork before serving.

OPTIONAL MICROWAVE PREPARATION:

Combine stock, rice, and salt to taste in a 1-quart microwave-safe dish. Cover dish with a fitted lid, and microwave on HIGH for 10 minutes. Reduce heat to 50% then microwave for an additional 10 minutes. Fluff rice with a fork before serving.

Buttery Brown Rice

I should mention that I cook this rice at least twice a month. I LOVE IT!

¼ cup butter

1 onion, diced

1 cup uncooked rice

2 cans beef consommé

Melt butter in a large skillet. Add onions and rice, and sauté over medium-high heat, stirring constantly for 7–8 minutes or until rice has browned. Add rice mixture and beef consommé to a 1.5-quart casserole dish, and cover. Bake at 375° for 1 hour, or microwave on HIGH for 5 minutes, then continue microwaving for 15 minutes at 50% power. Keep covered until ready to serve. Fluff with a fork before serving.

Creamy Parmesan Rice

You know those boxes of flavored rice you get at the grocery store? Sometimes I buy them because they're so easy, but I thought, you know . . . I could make that. So I did! Rice? Check! Milk? Check! Garlic? Check! Parmesan? Check! I threw everything together and hoped for the best. And it was! It was the best!

1 tablespoon minced garlic

4 tablespoons butter

1 cup uncooked white rice

1 cup water

1 cup 2% milk

½ teaspoon salt

⅓ cup grated Parmesan cheese

½ teaspoon parsley flakes

Sauté garlic in butter in a medium-size saucepan over medium heat until fragrant (3–4 minutes). Add rice, and stir to coat in butter. Add water, milk, and salt; bring to a boil. Simmer, covered, until rice is tender. (Don't mess around with your rice too much; just stir occasionally to make sure it's not sticking to the bottom.) Stir in Parmesan and parsley. If you like yours creamier, add a splash of milk. Add more salt, if necessary. Cover, turn off heat, and let rest 5 minutes. Enjoy!

Poultry

Let me just go on the record now and say that nothing can replace the flavor of good ol' coal-grilled barbequed chicken. And, yes, I know that by cooking it in the oven, I really shouldn't call it Oven Barbequed Chicken. Just work with me here. It looks, tastes, smells, and eats an awful lot like real barbequed chicken. Except it's EASY and requires no tending to, flipping, sweating, or gnat-swatting. Plus, come about July or so, it gets to be about 437 degrees here in South Carolina in the middle of the afternoon, and I just ain't interested enough in it to endure a heat stroke.

Slow Cooker Pulled Chicken

We served this Slow Cooker Pulled Chicken on buns like barbeque sandwiches and had a few different sauces to choose from. This is a great recipe to make when company's coming. You can throw the shredded chicken back into the slow cooker, pour a little of the cooking liquid over it to keep it moist, and have supper on stand-by.

1 (6- to 7-pound) chicken

3–4 tablespoons Chicken Scratch (see page 112)

2 small onions, peeled (optional)

Barbeque sauce (optional)

Wash chicken and pat dry with paper towels. Season all over with Chicken Scratch. Stuff onions inside chicken, if using. Place chicken in a slow cooker (without water); cook on LOW for 8–10 hours, or on HIGH for 5–6 hours. Turn slow cooker off, and allow chicken to rest for 30–45 minutes, covered.

Remove chicken to platter, using tongs or slotted spoon. Reserve broth for Greasy Rice (see page 107), if desired. Remove meat from chicken, and pull/shred into bite-sized pieces.

Serve on buns with barbeque sauce to make Pulled Chicken Sandwiches, or serve as-is with barbeque sauce on the side, if desired.

Slow Cooker Pulled Chicken

Chicken Scratch

This is a seasoning mix I came up with years ago that I use each and every time I cook chicken.

3 tablespoons salt

3 tablespoons paprika

3 tablespoons garlic powder

1 tablespoon dried thyme

1 tablespoon white pepper

1 tablespoon black pepper

1 tablespoon cayenne pepper

1 tablespoon onion powder

Mix all ingredients together, and store in an airtight container. I keep mine in a large used spice container that still has its shaker top for easy use. Season chicken or other poultry LIBERALLY (this is made with less than 25% salt, so you can rock it out!).

Oven Barbequed Chicken

Let me just go on the record now and say that nothing can replace the flavor of good ol' coal-grilled barbequed chicken. And, yes, I know that by cooking it in the oven, I really can't call it barbequed. Just work with me here. It looks, tastes, smells, and eats an awful lot like real barbequed chicken. Except it's EASY and requires no tending to, flipping, sweating, or gnat-swatting. Plus, come about July or so, it gets to be about 437 degrees here in South Carolina in the middle of the afternoon, and I just ain't interested enough in it to endure a heat stroke.

10 chicken legs or thighs

1 tablespoon olive oil

2–3 tablespoons Chicken Scratch (see page 112)

¾ cup barbeque sauce of choice

NOTE:
You can use any bone-in, skin-on chicken pieces, but dark meat works best with this low-and-slow cooking method (there's enough fat and skin to keep chicken from drying out). Reduce cooking time, if using chicken breasts, checking to see if they're done after about 1½ hours.

Place chicken in a large bowl. Add olive oil and Chicken Scratch, and toss to coat. (Do this with your hands, so you can make sure chicken is thoroughly and evenly covered.) Spray a 17x24-inch baking pan (or 2 standard-size baking sheets) with cooking spray. Arrange chicken pieces evenly on pan(s). Cook at 325° for 1 hour and 45 minutes. Baste with barbeque sauce, then return to oven, and cook for an additional 15 minutes.

Smoky Mountain Chicken

I don't know if they still serve it, but years ago at the circa 1994 Dillard House in Georgia, I had the Smoky Mountain Chicken and fell in love. I have never had it since, but I've never forgotten it either, so I set out to re-create it.

4 large boneless, skinless chicken breasts

1 cup Italian dressing

Salt and pepper to taste

½ cup barbeque sauce

20–24 very thin slices smoked ham

4 slices Muenster or provolone cheese

½ cup diced scallions

½ cup diced tomatoes

1 lime

Marinate chicken in Italian dressing for 4–6 hours. Season liberally with salt and pepper; grill low and slow, until just done (about 30 minutes). Baste generously with barbeque sauce on both sides during last 5 minutes of cook time. Top each piece with 5–6 slices of ham and 1 piece of cheese.

Remove chicken to a baking sheet, and bake at 350° until cheese is melted (or if using a gas grill, turn off heat, and cover until cheese is melted). Toss scallions and tomatoes with juice from the lime; sprinkle over chicken pieces when ready to serve. Serve with extra barbeque sauce on the side (or if you're feeling really snazzy, drizzle the chicken with barbeque sauce before adding the tomatoes and onions).

NOTE:

When cooking boneless, skinless chicken breasts, I usually fold the thin edges under before placing on grill to create an even thickness to ensure it doesn't dry out (as boneless, skinless chicken is prone to do). You can also just bake or pan-fry the chicken, if you don't feel like grilling it.

Chicken Cordon Bleu Casserole

This is delicious, and the leftovers are even better the next day!

½ pound penne pasta

1 pint half-and-half

1 (8-ounce) block cream cheese, softened

¼ teaspoon white pepper

¼ teaspoon dried thyme, or ½ teaspoon chopped fresh thyme

¼ teaspoon cayenne pepper

½ teaspoon granulated garlic

1 teaspoon salt

1 tablespoon Dijon mustard

1 pound fully cooked ham cubes (2–3 cups)

2 large chicken breasts, cooked and cubed (2–3 cups)

8 ounces Swiss cheese, shredded (2 cups)

PANKO TOPPING:

1¾ cups panko bread crumbs

¼ teaspoon salt

¼ teaspoon granulated garlic

1 tablespoon dried parsley (optional)

6 tablespoons butter, melted

Spray a 9x13-inch baking dish with cooking spray; set aside. Cook pasta al dente per package instructions in liberally salted water; drain and set aside. Heat and stir next 8 ingredients over medium heat until cream cheese is melted and mixture is smooth. In a large bowl, combine cooked pasta, ham, chicken, and cream sauce; fold in Swiss cheese. Pour into baking dish.

In medium bowl, combine Panko Topping ingredients. Sprinkle over casserole. Bake, uncovered, at 350° for 30 minutes or until topping is light golden brown.

NOTE:
If you can't find cooked ham cubes, just buy a ham steak, trim the fat, and cut it into cubes.

Crispy Baked Chicken Wings

Ultimately, to get crispy wings from the oven, you have to desiccate them (dry them out first). You do this by coating them in baking soda (a natural desiccant) and leaving them in the refrigerator, uncovered, for several hours (refrigerators dehydrate).

4 pounds chicken wing sections

1 tablespoon new baking soda

Black pepper

SWEET ASIAN HOT WING SAUCE:

(Makes enough for about 30 wings)

⅔ cup hot sauce (Texas Pete or Frank's)

⅔ cup brown sugar

½ cup soy sauce

1–2 cloves garlic, smashed

Carefully dry chicken wings with clean kitchen towels or paper towels (really do a good job at this—there can't be any moisture left on the wings). Arrange wings on cooling racks in a single layer. Sprinkle with half of the baking soda (I added mine to an empty spice shaker to make easy work of the sprinkling). Flip wings, and sprinkle other side with remainder of baking soda. Place wings, on racks, uncovered, in the refrigerator for 18–24 hours.

Season wings with black pepper (do not add salt—the baking soda is plenty salty); arrange in a single layer on 1 extra large, or 2 normal, baking pans sprayed with cooking spray. Bake at 450° for 15 minutes. Flip wings; continue baking 15–20 minutes longer, until crispy and golden brown. Toss wings with wing sauce, and serve immediately.

Combine Sweet Asian Hot Wing Sauce ingredients in a small saucepan, and simmer over medium heat for 20 minutes. Discard garlic.

VARIATION:
Add fresh ginger and red pepper flakes, if desired.

Crispy Baked Chicken Wings

Pan-Fried Chicken Tenders

Pan-frying allows you to use just enough oil to cook these tenders on each side, and you don't have to submerge them in oil, which is fattening and messy.

1 pound chicken tenderloins

2 tablespoons Chicken Scratch, divided (see page 112)

1 egg

¼ cup milk

¼ cup hot sauce

1 cup all-purpose flour

¼ teaspoon black pepper

¼ teaspoon dry mustard

Vegetable oil

Season chicken with 1 tablespoon Chicken Scratch; set aside. Whisk egg, milk, and hot sauce in a shallow bowl; set aside. Combine remaining 1 tablespoon Chicken Scratch, flour, black pepper, and dry mustard in another shallow bowl; set aside.

Working in batches, dip seasoned chicken in egg wash, then toss to coat in flour mixture. Place chicken on a cooling rack or plate lined with wax paper, and refrigerate until ready to use. Allowing them to rest a bit will help the breading stick to the chicken tenders.

Heat 1 inch vegetable oil in a large cast-iron skillet until temperature reaches 335°–340°. Pan-fry chicken until golden brown and crispy (about 5 minutes), turning once; drain on cooling rack or paper towels.

Stuffed Chicken with Gravy

This casserole is the mother of easy recipes. It's so easy, it's almost embarrassing.

- **1 (6-ounce) box chicken stuffing mix (or cornbread stuffing)**
- **6 boneless, skinless chicken thighs**
- **Salt, pepper, and granulated garlic to taste**
- **1 (12-ounce) jar chicken gravy**

NOTE:

Can substitute chicken breast cutlets, if desired, but I think the thighs are amazingly flavorful and moist. They're kinda my favorite weeknight protein right now.

Prepare stuffing mix per package instructions, cover, and set aside. Spray a 9x13-inch casserole dish with cooking spray. Trim excess fat from chicken, then season both sides with salt, pepper, and garlic. Place about ¼ cup of stuffing mix on each piece of chicken, then wrap sides around to create a little bundle. Place bundles in casserole dish. Spoon remaining stuffing into dish around chicken bundles. Cover dish with aluminum foil, and bake at 375° for 30 minutes.

Remove from oven; remove aluminum foil, then pour gravy (as much as you like) over chicken and stuffing. Continue cooking, uncovered, 10–15 more minutes or until chicken is cooked through. Boom! Done.

Honey Dijon Chicken Breasts

4 boneless, skinless chicken breasts

1 tablespoon olive oil

1 tablespoon Dijon mustard

1 tablespoon honey, plus more for dipping or drizzle

1–2 cloves garlic, minced

½ teaspoon salt

½ teaspoon pepper

½ teaspoon paprika

Rinse chicken breasts, and pat dry with paper towels, then add to a medium-size bowl. In a separate bowl, combine remaining ingredients, and mix well. Add honey mixture to chicken, and combine by hand until chicken is evenly coated.

Spray a 9x13-inch baking dish with cooking spray, add chicken, and cover tightly with aluminum foil. Bake at 375° for 15 minutes. Remove aluminum foil, and continue cooking for approximately 15 more minutes or until chicken is done.

Serve with a small cup of honey for dipping, or drizzle cooked chicken with a little more honey.

Honey Garlic Chicken

A friend of mine makes a chicken dish in the slow cooker using honey garlic sauce. I've been craving it, so I decided to try to re-create it. And I totally did. And it was AH-MA-ZING! And we totally ate every last bit of it. And we all had drum-tight, fat puppy bellies when supper was over.

3 pounds boneless, skinless chicken thighs

Black pepper

1 cup honey

6–7 garlic cloves, minced

⅔ cup soy sauce

3 tablespoons ketchup

½ teaspoon red pepper flakes

1 bunch green onions, finely diced

2 tablespoons cornstarch

½ cup water

Season chicken liberally with black pepper, and place in slow cooker.

Combine honey, garlic, soy sauce, ketchup, and red pepper in a medium-size bowl, and whisk until thoroughly incorporated. Add green onions (reserve some for garnish, if desired); stir. Pour honey mixture over chicken; cook, covered, on HIGH for 3–4 hours (or LOW for 5–6 hours), until chicken is cooked through and tender.

Remove chicken from slow cooker; cover to keep moist. Increase temperature to HIGH, and replace lid. Add cornstarch to a small bowl or cup, then slowly add water; stir until smooth. Add cornstarch slurry to slow cooker, cover, and heat until sauce thickens (about 30 minutes).

Chop chicken into bite-sized pieces, and add back to slow cooker. Gently stir to coat with sauce. Reduce heat to WARM until ready to serve. Garnish with chopped green onions, if desired. Serve over white rice, if desired. Steamed, fresh broccoli goes really well with this, too!

Smothered Cheesy Chicken

When I made this the first time, I loved it. I mean like I loved it, loved it. There was not one bit of this left when we were done. The kids were using their bread to sop up the cheesy bits of potatoes from the bottom of the dish. I didn't even have to rinse the casserole before I put it in the dishwasher. The bottom layer is like potatoes au gratin then it's topped with tender, flavorful chicken and bacon and all smothered in cheese. I mean, come on! Talk about a home run for your taste buds! And the best part? It's all wrapped up in a perfect casserole.

1 (10¾-ounce) can Cheddar cheese soup

1¼ cups milk

4–5 medium russet potatoes, washed, peeled, and cut into slices about ¼ inch thick

8–10 slices bacon, sliced into ½-inch strips

8 chicken breast tenderloins (about 1½ pounds)

4 ounces cheese, shredded (1 cup)

Salt and pepper to taste

NOTE:
I used Monterey Jack cheese because I thought the white cheese would be a nice contrast to the Cheddar soup mixture, but feel free to use whatever's handy!

Preheat oven to 350°. Spray bottom and sides of 9x13-inch baking dish with cooking spray.

Whisk cheese soup and milk until smooth. Reserve 1 cup cheese soup mixture to use later. Spoon ¼ of cheese soup mixture into bottom of prepared dish. Add a layer of potato slices. Season with salt and pepper. Spoon another ¼ of soup mixture over potatoes. Repeat process 2 more times so that you have 3 layers topped with soup mixture and seasoned. Cover dish tightly with aluminum foil, and bake for 30 minutes.

Cook bacon in skillet over medium-high heat until browned and crispy. Remove bacon from skillet; set aside. Season chicken with salt and pepper (or Chicken Scratch, see page 112), then sear in bacon drippings over until lightly browned; set aside.

Remove dish from oven, and uncover. Arrange chicken on top of potatoes, and pour reserved 1 cup cheese soup mixture over chicken. Cover tightly again, and cook 30 more minutes. Remove dish from oven, and uncover. Sprinkle evenly with shredded cheese, then top with bacon. Return to oven, and cook, uncovered, until cheese is melted and bubbly.

Smothered Cheesy Chicken

Nanny's Chicken and Dumplings

DUMPLINGS:

2 cups all-purpose flour

¾ teaspoon baking powder

½ teaspoon salt

4 tablespoons butter

¾ cup milk

CHICKEN:

1 large chicken

2 teaspoons salt

1 teaspoon pepper

1 teaspoon garlic powder

½ teaspoon dried thyme

1 bay leaf

4 celery stalks, quartered

4 carrots, quartered

1 onion, quartered

8 cups water

4–6 boiled eggs, sliced

Mix flour, baking powder, and salt in large bowl. Cut butter into flour mixture with a fork or pastry cutter (or pulse in a food processor) until mixture is the consistency of coarse meal. Gently stir in milk until just combined (do not overwork the dough). Turn dough out onto a floured surface, and roll out to desired thickness. Add flour to top of dough as you roll them out—you want these to have a good amount of flour on both sides, as the flour will thicken the broth. Using a pizza cutter or sharp knife; cut dough into 1x2-inch strips. Set aside while you cook your stock.

Add all Chicken ingredients, except boiled eggs, to a large stock pot, cover, and heat on medium-high heat until simmering. Once simmering, reduce heat to medium low, and simmer for 1½ hours.

Remove chicken from stock. Once cool enough to handle, pull the chicken from the bones, discarding skin, bones, etc. Cover chicken, and set aside.

Strain stock through a mesh strainer to remove the vegetables and bay leaf. Add stock back to pot, and heat over medium-high heat until boiling. Add Dumplings, one at a time, cover, and cook 5 minutes, stirring occasionally. Reduce heat to medium low; add chicken. Continue cooking, covered, until dumplings are tender. Add more salt and pepper, if necessary.

Stir in boiled eggs, cover, remove from heat, and let rest 20 minutes before serving.

One-Pan Roasted Chicken and Potato Bake

I looooove to entertain. Feeding people makes me happy. When the weather's nice, sometimes I just want to be outside and not have to fuss too much over whatever we're eating. On one of those nice days, I decided to just throw a bunch of good stuff in a pan and hope for the best! I'm thinking of classifying this as a no-fail recipe because the truth is, despite my sipping on sangria, it still came out perfectly! I doubled this recipe, and four adults and five children ate every single last flippin' bit of it. GONE!

10–12 chicken legs or thighs (bone-in, skin-on)

6 tablespoons olive oil, divided

5 tablespoons Chicken Scratch, divided (see page 112)

6–8 Yukon gold potatoes

1 large onion

1 sweet bell pepper (I used an orange one)

In a large bowl, toss chicken with 3 tablespoons olive oil. Add 2 tablespoons Chicken Scratch, and mix with hands until seasoning is evenly distributed. Spray a 13x18-inch baking pan (or 2 standard-size cookie sheets) with cooking spray; arrange chicken on pan. Bake, uncovered, at 300° for 1 hour.

Wash potatoes, cut into cubes (leave skin on), and add to a large bowl. Cut onion and bell pepper into chunks, and add to potatoes with remaining olive oil and Chicken Scratch; toss to coat. Set aside.

Remove chicken from oven, and pour off liquid. Add vegetables to pan around chicken. Return to oven, and continue baking, uncovered, at 300° for 1 hour.

Jive Turkey and Homemade Gravy

Over the years, I've come up with what I think is the best turkey recipe EVER! You're going to look at the length of this recipe and think, DANG this is involved! But it's really not. Read the entire recipe through so there are no surprises (start the Brine the day before). And seriously, you're prolly only going to cook this once a year so why not go all out!

BRINE:

2 gallons water, divided

4 onions, quartered

8 carrots, chopped

8 celery stalks, chopped

4 tablespoons dried thyme

4 tablespoons dried rosemary

1 cup table salt

½ cup sugar

1 (18-pound) turkey, reserve neck and giblets

NOTE:
If you're cooking a larger turkey and need more Brine, use ½ cup salt and ¼ cup sugar for every gallon of water needed to cover the turkey.

For the Brine, bring 2 quarts water to a boil in a large saucepan. Add onions, carrots, and celery; reduce heat to medium low, cover, and simmer for 1 hour. Remove from heat; add thyme and rosemary. Cover, and cool to room temperature. Once cool, add to a large stock pot. Add remaining water (6 quarts), salt, and sugar to vegetable stock; stir to dissolve sugar.

Add turkey to the Brine. Cover, and refrigerate overnight (at least 12–24 hours).

Remove turkey from Brine; rinse inside and out. Tie legs together with kitchen string (or tuck them back into the skin). Place turkey BREAST-SIDE DOWN on a roasting rack (if you don't have a roasting rack, rough-chop onions, celery, and carrots, and place on bottom of pan so turkey can rest on veggies and not on bottom of pan).

JIVE TURKEY SEASONING:

¾ teaspoon salt

1 teaspoon paprika

1 teaspoon garlic powder

1 teaspoon dried thyme

1 teaspoon dried sage

1 teaspoon black pepper

1 teaspoon cayenne pepper

1 teaspoon onion powder

TURKEY GRAVY:

4 tablespoons unsalted butter

¼ cup all-purpose flour

4 cups turkey stock/chicken broth

Salt and pepper to taste

Season turkey with ½ the Jive Turkey Seasoning. Place in a baking pan, and add just enough water to cover bottom of pan. Bake, uncovered, at 325° for 1½ hours, basting twice. Remove from oven. Flip the turkey so that it is setting BREAST-SIDE UP in pan. Baste with pan juices, and season with remaining Jive Turkey Seasoning. Return to oven, and cook 3 more hours, or until a meat thermometer registers 165° and skin is golden brown, basting every 30 minutes.

Remove from oven. Remove turkey from pan (reserving pan juices for gravy), cover loosely with aluminum foil, and allow turkey to rest for 20 minutes before carving.

Add water to cover turkey neck and giblets (pull the meat off the neck and chop with giblets); cook until meat is done; reserve turkey stock. Pour reserved pan juices through a mesh strainer. Combine reserved pan juices with reserved homemade stock (or chicken broth) to measure 4 cups liquid (the fat will settle on the top; pour off the fat, if possible). Set aside.

For the gravy, melt butter in a medium saucepan over medium-high heat. Add flour, and whisk to incorporate. Cook and whisk 2–3 minutes, until roux is light brown. Add stock/broth, and whisk 2–3 minutes, until gravy starts to thicken. Add salt and pepper (the pan juices from the Jive Turkey are on the salty side from the Brine, so taste first before adding salt). Add chopped neck meat and giblets. Reduce heat to medium low, and cook until gravy has reduced and thickened.

Homemade Shake and Bake

I can't hear the words "shake and bake" without thinking about Talladega Nights. *And I have a huge fluffy black cat named Ricky Bobby. Enough about me already!*

3 cups plain dried bread crumbs

1 tablespoon salt

1 tablespoon granulated garlic

2 teaspoons onion powder

2 teaspoons paprika

1 teaspoon dried parsley

1 teaspoon dried thyme

1 teaspoon black pepper

1 teaspoon chili powder

¼ cup vegetable oil

Combine bread crumbs and seasonings, and mix well. Slowly whisk in vegetable oil until thoroughly combined. Divide mixture evenly into 4 zip-top bags. Store in freezer for up to 1 year. Bring to room temperature before using.

TO PREPARE MEAT:

Place uncooked chicken or pork, one piece at a time (for chicken nuggets or strips, add 3–4 pieces at a time), in zip-top bag of Shake and Bake. Seal bag, and shake until meat is thoroughly coated. Lightly spray a baking pan with cooking spray, arrange pieces evenly, at least 1 inch apart.

COOKING TEMPS AND TIMES:

Whole, bone-in chicken pieces: 375° for 35–45 minutes, till chicken is cooked through and coating is crunchy.

Whole, boneless chicken breasts: 400° for 25–30 minutes, till chicken is cooked through and coating is crunchy.

Chicken strips or nuggets: 400° for 20–25 minutes, till chicken is cooked through and coating is crunchy.

Bone-in pork chops: 375° for 35–45 minutes, till pork is cooked through and coating is crunchy.

Boneless pork chops: 400° for 25–30 minutes, till pork is cooked through and coating is crunchy.

Seafood

Remember the first time you saw Twilight *and you walked out of the theater in a glittery daze and thought to yourself, "Man I wonder what's in Harry Clearwater's Fish Fry?" No? Well, I did! So I decided I would try to create a recipe for a fish fry for my Southern Fried Fish. Serve with a big basket of homemade Hush Puppies (see page 39) for an authentic southern fish-fry experience.*

Southern Shrimp and Grits

2 cups chicken broth

2 cups milk

6 tablespoons butter

¾ teaspoon salt

½ teaspoon pepper

¾ cup old-fashioned grits

1 cup (4 ounces) shredded
   Cheddar cheese

1 pound uncooked medium
   shrimp, peeled

1 tablespoon hot sauce

2 teaspoons Cajun or
   blackening seasoning

8 thick-sliced strips bacon

3 garlic cloves, minced

4 green onions, chopped

Combine first 5 ingredients in a large saucepan, and bring to a boil over high heat. Whisk in grits; reduce heat to low, cover tightly, and simmer for 1 hour, whisking every 10–15 minutes. Add cheese, and stir until thoroughly incorporated. Keep warm until ready to serve.

Toss shrimp with hot sauce and Cajun seasoning; set aside. Sauté bacon in a large skillet over medium-high heat until browned and crisp. Add garlic and shrimp, and sauté until shrimp turn pink, 3–5 minutes. Ladle grits into a bowl, and top with shrimp mixture. Garnish with chopped green onions.

NOTE:
For thinner grits, just whisk in a bit of warm milk.

Southern Shrimp and Grits

Low-Country Shrimp Boil

2 (3-ounce) boxes crab boil seasoning

¼ cup Old Bay Seasoning

½ cup hot sauce

3 bay leaves

4 pounds small red potatoes

6 quarts water

4 pounds smoked sausage, cut into 3-inch pieces

6–8 ears fresh corn, halved

4 lemons, halved

4 pounds unpeeled shrimp

COCKTAIL SAUCE:

1 cup ketchup

¼ cup prepared horseradish (or more to taste)

1 teaspoon lemon juice

Combine crab boil, Old Bay, hot sauce, bay leaves, potatoes, and water in a large pot, and bring to a boil. Cover, reduce to a simmer, and cook potatoes 15 minutes. (I use an elongated pot that fits over 2 burners on the stove, but you can also cook with an outdoor propane cooker. Do not try to cook this using only 1 standard stove burner.)

Add sausage, corn, and lemons, and return to a boil. Cover, reduce to a simmer, and cook 10 additional minutes or until potatoes are fork-tender.

Add shrimp, cover, and turn off heat. Leave dish covered for 5 minutes, or until shrimp turn pink and are cooked through. Drain liquid, then serve with Cocktail Sauce (often served directly on a paper-lined outdoor table).

Combine Cocktail Sauce ingredients, and refrigerate until ready to serve.

Grilled Chipotle Shrimp with Cilantro Cream Sauce

This is a dish of mine that won a Taste of Home *recipe contest.*

GRILLED CHIPOTLE SHRIMP:

¼ cup brown sugar

2 chipotle peppers, chopped

¼ cup adobo sauce (from can of chipotle peppers)

6 garlic cloves, minced

2 tablespoons water

2 tablespoons lime juice

1 tablespoon olive oil

¼ teaspoon salt

2 pounds large shrimp, peeled and deveined

CILANTRO CREAM SAUCE:

1 cup sour cream

⅓ cup minced fresh cilantro

2 garlic cloves, minced

1½ teaspoons grated lime peel

¼ teaspoon salt

In a small saucepan, bring all ingredients except shrimp to a boil. Reduce heat; cook and stir 2 minutes longer. Remove from heat; cool completely. Transfer mixture to a large re-sealable plastic bag. Add the shrimp; seal bag and turn to coat. Refrigerate for 2 hours.

Drain, and discard marinade. Thread shrimp onto skewers, then grill or broil 2–3 minutes on each side (or until no longer pink). Serve with Cilantro Cream Sauce for dipping.

Combine the sauce ingredients; chill until serving.

Butter Baked Shrimp with Lemon

½ cup (1 stick) butter, melted

2 lemons, sliced

1 pound unpeeled shrimp

1 tablespoon Old Bay
    Seasoning

Pour melted butter into a 9x13-inch baking dish. Arrange lemon slices evenly over melted butter. Arrange shrimp evenly over lemon slices. Generously sprinkle Old Bay over unpeeled shrimp. Bake at 350° for approximately 10 minutes or until shrimp turn pink and are cooked through. Strain butter and lemons from pan, and serve as a dipping sauce for shrimp.

Easy Shrimp Tacos

8–10 small flour tortillas

1 pound fried shrimp

1 (10-ounce) bag shredded
    coleslaw mix with dressing,
    prepared

¾ cup chopped cilantro

1 jalapeño, seeded and diced

8–10 lime wedges

Wrap tortillas in aluminum foil, and heat at 350° for 5 minutes or until heated through.

Assemble tacos by placing 3–4 shrimp in each tortilla. Top shrimp with slaw, cilantro, and jalapeño. Squeeze lime juice over tacos just before eating.

Southern Fried Shrimp

1 cup buttermilk

2 teaspoons hot sauce

2 pounds large shrimp, peeled and deveined

1½ cups all-purpose flour

½ cup cornmeal

1 tablespoon salt

1 tablespoon pepper

1 teaspoon onion powder

1 teaspoon cayenne pepper

Oil for frying

Add buttermilk and hot sauce to a large bowl, and stir to combine. Add shrimp to buttermilk; set aside. Add flour, cornmeal, salt, pepper, onion powder, and cayenne pepper to a large paper bag. Fold bag closed, then shake to combine.

Drain buttermilk mixture from shrimp. Add shrimp to the paper bag filled with flour mixture, fold to close, and shake to coat shrimp.

Add 3–4 inches of oil to a medium pot, and heat over medium-high heat until temperature reaches 350°. Fry shrimp in hot oil until golden brown. Do not overcrowd the pan; cook in batches, if necessary.

Charleston Crab Cakes

1 pound blue crabmeat

1 stalk celery, finely diced

1 small onion, finely diced

1 teaspoon yellow mustard

1½ tablespoons mayonnaise

1 egg, beaten

1 tablespoon parsley

½ teaspoon paprika

1 tablespoon Old Bay
   Seasoning

2 slices bread, cut into small
   cubes

Melted butter

Lemon wedges (optional)

Combine crabmeat, celery, and onion in a medium bowl; set aside. In a small bowl, add mustard, mayonnaise, egg, parsley, paprika, and Old Bay Seasoning, and mix until thoroughly combined. Add mustard mixture and bread cubes to crab mixture, and toss until just combined.

Brush the insides of a 12-muffin muffin tin with melted butter. Divide crab mixture evenly into muffin tin (you'll get anywhere from 10–12 crab cakes, depending on how big you want them). Bake at 375° for 30 minutes or until golden brown. Let crab cakes rest 5 minutes in the muffin tin. Slide a knife around the edges of each crab cake to loosen, then remove to a serving platter.

Squeeze fresh lemon juice over crab cakes when serving, if desired.

VARIATION:
You can also pan-fry these in vegetable oil, if preferred.

Charleston Crab Cakes

Blackened Fish

BLACKENING SEASONING:

1 tablespoon paprika

2 teaspoons salt

1 teaspoon onion powder

1 teaspoon granulated garlic

1 teaspoon cayenne pepper

½ teaspoon white pepper

½ teaspoon dried thyme leaves

½ teaspoon dried oregano leaves

¾ teaspoon black pepper

FISH:

6–8 thick fish fillets (such as bass, red fish, or snapper)

¼ cup butter, melted

Vegetable oil

Lemon juice

Heat a large cast-iron skillet over medium-high heat for 10 minutes. Meanwhile, mix all ingredients for Blackening Seasoning in a pie plate or other deep dish.

Dip each fish fillet in melted butter, then dredge on both sides in Blackening Seasoning. Drizzle vegetable oil in hot skillet. Cook fillets for 2–3 minutes on each side or until cooked through. Drizzle with fresh lemon juice to serve.

Southern Fried Fish

Remember the first time you saw Twilight *and you walked out of the theater in a glittery daze and thought to yourself, "Man I wonder what's in Harry Clearwater's Fish Fry?" No? Well, I did! So I decided I would try to create a recipe for a fish fry. Serve with a big basket of homemade Hush Puppies (see page 39) for an authentic southern fish-fry experience.*

SOUTH YOUR MOUTH FISH FRY:

1½ cups medium ground cornmeal

½ cup all-purpose flour

1 tablespoon salt

1 tablespoon onion powder

1 tablespoon black pepper

2 teaspoons paprika

FISH:

Vegetable oil

2 pounds white fish

Salt and pepper to taste

1 cup buttermilk

½ cup hot sauce

Mix all fish fry ingredients, and store in an airtight container. Use for frying fish or shellfish.

Heat a minimum of 4 inches of oil in a deep skillet or wide pan to 350° (medium-high heat). Season fish with salt and pepper. In a medium bowl, mix buttermilk and hot sauce. Dip fish,1 piece at a time, in buttermilk mixture, and shake off all excess liquid. Dredge fish in fish fry, and immediately add to hot oil. Cook until golden brown, and remove to a plate or pan lined with paper towels.

You may use any flaky, white fish you prefer (crappy, bream, catfish, tilapia, flounder, etc.). I actually used swai fillets. I had no idea what swai was, but it was only a few bucks for a 2–pound package so I thought . . . meh? If you like catfish, you will LOVE swai. I found it to be almost identical to catfish.

NOTE:
If using self-rising cornmeal, increase amount to 2 cups, and omit flour.

Easy Grilled Fish Kebabs

2 pounds halibut or mahi mahi
    fillets

1½ cups Italian dressing

Salt and pepper to taste

Cut fillets into 1½- to 2-inch squares, then add to a large zip-top bag with Italian dressing. Marinate 1–2 hours (no longer than 2 hours).

Thread fish onto skewers, and discard marinade. Season kebabs with salt and pepper, then grill over medium heat (about 350°) for 10–12 minutes, or until fish is cooked through, turning to cook on each side.

Easy Broiled Tilapia

Get ready for the easiest tilapia recipe ever! It's easy, breezy, lemon-squeezy delicious.

2 tablespoons fresh lemon
    juice

¼ cup butter

½ teaspoon paprika

8 tilapia fillets

Salt to taste

NOTE:
You could use just about any other type of fish fillet.

Line a 9x13-inch baking pan with aluminum foil (or don't . . . it just makes for easy cleaning). Add lemon juice, butter, and paprika to a small bowl. Place bowl in microwave, and heat until butter is melted. Stir well. Add butter mixture to baking pan. Place tilapia fillets in butter mixture, and sprinkle with salt. Flip each fillet, and season with salt again (so that both sides of fillets are coated with butter and seasoned with salt).

Place baking pan on top rack of oven, and broil on high with oven door closed for 5 minutes. Remove from oven, and baste fillets with butter mixture from the pan. Return to oven, and continue broiling with oven door open until fillets are sizzling and slightly browned.

Potato Chip Crusted Cod

5–6 cod fillets (about 1 inch thick)

Salt and pepper to taste

1 (6-ounce) bag salt and vinegar potato chips

2 eggs, well beaten

2 tablespoons hot sauce

Blot fish fillets dry with paper towels, then season both sides with salt and pepper; set aside.

Crush potato chips. (I used a food processor, which made quick work of the task, and resulted in nice even-sized crumbs.) Place potato chip crumbs in a shallow dish; set aside. In another shallow dish, beat eggs with hot sauce; set aside. Line a baking sheet with aluminum foil. Place baking rack atop foil, then spray with cooking spray; set aside.

Dip 1 fillet in egg wash, and let excess drip off. Place fillet in potato chips, and press down to get a good coating. Flip the fillet, and coat the other side as well. Use a spoon or fork to bring potato chips up to coat the edges of the fillet. Arrange fillets on the prepared baking rack. Rinse, and repeat until all fillets are coated.

If you don't have a baking rack, just cook fillets on a baking sheet sprayed with cooking spray, but do not coat the bottom of the fillets with chips. (The fish will put off moisture as it cooks, which will make for a soggy mess on the bottom.) Bake fillets at 400° for 20 minutes, or until fish is cooked through and potato chip coating is golden brown. Cool for 5–10 minutes before serving.

Daddy's Fish Nuggets

All Daddy does is lightly dust the fish nuggets with fish fry, and plop them in some hot oil, and they turn out great every time!

2 pounds cod or catfish fillets, cut into 1-inch nuggets

Salt to taste

2 cups South Your Mouth Fish Fry (Page 145)

Vegetable oil

Season fish nuggets lightly with salt. Add fish nuggets and South Your Mouth Fish Fry to a large, lidded plastic container or brown paper bag, and shake to coat. Shake off excess, then add fish to deep fryer with enough hot oil (heated to 350°) to cover fish; cook until golden brown. Remove to a cooling rack or pan lined with paper towels to drain. Serve hot.

Salt and Pepper Pan-Fried Catfish

4 catfish fillets

1 teaspoon salt

1 teaspoon lemon pepper

½ teaspoon coarse-ground black pepper

3–4 tablespoons all-purpose flour

3 tablespoons real butter

3 tablespoons vegetable oil

TARTAR SAUCE:

1 cup mayonnaise

1 medium dill pickle, diced (about ⅓ cup)

½ teaspoon dried dill

Blot fish dry with paper towels, then season with salt, lemon pepper, and coarse-ground black pepper. Place flour in a pie plate or other deep dish, then dredge each fillet in flour; set aside. (The flour won't stick much to the fish, which is what we want—only a dusting of flour.)

Heat butter (for flavor) and vegetable oil (for heat resistance) in a large nonstick skillet over medium-high heat. Cook catfish for 4–5 minutes on each side, or until golden brown and crispy. Serve with Tartar Sauce.

Combine Tartar Sauce ingredients, and refrigerate until ready to serve.

Oven-Barbequed Salmon

¼ cup orange juice

Juice from 1 lemon

4–6 salmon fillets

2 tablespoons brown sugar

1 tablespoon chili powder

1 tablespoon paprika

½ teaspoon cumin

½ teaspoon garlic powder

½ teaspoon salt

Combine orange juice and lemon juice, and pour into a large zip-top bag. Add salmon fillets, and marinate 2–4 hours in refrigerator.

Cover a large baking sheet with aluminum foil, and spray liberally with cooking spray. Combine brown sugar and remaining ingredients, then add to a pie plate or other deep dish. Remove salmon fillets from marinade, and shake off any excess. Dredge fillets in spice mixture (on both sides), and place on prepared baking sheet. Bake at 425° for 15 minutes, or until salmon is done and flakes easily with a fork.

Old-School Salmon Patties

1 can salmon, bones and skin removed

2 teaspoons yellow mustard

1 egg, beaten

1 small onion, finely diced

¾ teaspoon Old Bay Seasoning

Dash of salt and pepper

¼ cup dried bread crumbs

Vegetable oil

Combine salmon, mustard, egg, onion, Old Bay, salt, and pepper, and stir with a fork until just combined. Add bread crumbs, and stir to incorporate. Shape into 6 patties. Add just enough vegetable oil to a large skillet to coat the bottom well. Heat over medium-high heat. Pan-fry salmon patties 3–4 minutes on each side, or until golden brown.

Meats

I think maybe a lot of you are just like me . . . you're crazy busy, and working with a limited budget, but still want to sit down with your family every night and eat supper. We have this Sweet and Tangy Smoked Sausage at least twice a month. I usually serve this with boiled potatoes and pork n' beans. Just good ol' blue collar grub made with good ol' working mama love. Enjoy!

Hamburger Steaks with Brown Gravy

Can you think of many things that are better than brown gravy? Honestly, I would choose a plate of rice and gravy with a side of black-eyed peas and fresh sliced tomatoes and cucumbers over filet mignon. I'm not even kidding!

HAMBURGER STEAKS:

1 pound ground beef

½ teaspoon salt

½ teaspoon pepper

½ teaspoon onion powder

½ teaspoon garlic powder

BROWN GRAVY:

2 tablespoons pan drippings

2 tablespoons flour

1¾ cups beef stock

Salt and pepper to taste

Crumble ground beef in a medium bowl, and add salt, pepper, onion powder, and garlic powder; mix by hand until seasoning is evenly distributed, taking care not to overwork the meat. Shape into 4 thin hamburger steaks (about ½ inch thick).

Heat a frying pan over medium-high heat until good and hot; cook steaks on each side 4–5 minutes, or until nicely seared. Remove steaks to a plate, and set aside (don't worry if they aren't cooked through; they will finish cooking in the gravy).

Reduce frying pan temperature to medium. Pour off pan drippings into a cup or bowl, then measure 2 tablespoons drippings back into the pan (add melted bacon grease or butter, if needed, to make 2 tablespoons). Add flour to pan, and whisk to incorporate. Continue cooking and whisking for 3–4 minutes, or until roux is medium brown. Add beef stock, and continue whisking for 2–3 minutes, or until gravy starts to thicken a little (gravy will be thin). Add salt and pepper to taste.

Add Hamburger Steaks to gravy, reduce heat to medium low, and continue cooking uncovered 10–15 minutes, or until meat juices run clear and gravy has reduced and thickened. Serve with white rice or mashed potatoes.

Hamburger Steaks with Cheddar and Caramelized Onions

1½ pounds ground beef

1 teaspoon salt

1 teaspoon pepper

½ teaspoon onion powder

½ teaspoon garlic powder

4 thick slices Cheddar cheese

1 large onion, peeled and sliced

⅓ cup barbeque sauce

Crumble ground beef in a medium bowl, and add salt, pepper, onion powder, and garlic powder; mix by hand until seasoning is evenly distributed, taking care not to overwork the meat. Shape into 4 thin hamburger steaks (about ½ inch thick). Heat a frying pan over medium-high heat. Once pan is good and hot, add hamburger steaks, and sear 3–4 minutes. Flip steaks, reduce heat to medium, and cook 5–6 minutes, or until juices run clear. Do not press down on steaks. Remove steaks from pan, and add 1 slice of Cheddar cheese to each. Increase heat to medium high, then add onion to pan drippings. Sauté onion until tender, then remove pan from heat. Add barbeque sauce to onion, and stir until thoroughly combined. When ready to serve, plate hamburger steaks, and top with onion.

My Best Meatloaf

I like a meatloaf that will slice, not crumble, because I really like meatloaf sandwiches. Pan-fry thick slices in a little oil until they've got a slight "crust" to them, then dress those bad boys like burgers.

2 eggs

1 teaspoon salt

1 teaspoon pepper

1 teaspoon garlic powder

1 teaspoon Italian seasoning

1 teaspoon chopped parsley

1 tablespoon Worcestershire

1 onion, grated

2¼ pounds ground beef

½ grated Parmesan cheese

½ cup dried bread crumbs

¼ cup ketchup

3 tablespoons barbeque sauce

Combine eggs, salt, pepper, garlic powder, Italian seasoning, parsley, Worcestershire, and onion in large bowl; mix well. Crumble ground beef into same bowl; add grated Parmesan and bread crumbs, and gently combine ingredients with hands, taking care not to overwork the meat (don't "squeeze" it through your fingers). Shape into a loaf (as best you can), and place mixture into loaf pan to finish shaping, patting it until it is uniform in size.

Bake at 425° for 15 minutes (to sear) then reduce heat to 350°, and continue cooking for 1 hour. Combine ketchup and barbeque sauce. Baste meatloaf with ketchup mixture; cook for 10 more minutes. Remove meatloaf from oven, cover loosely with aluminum foil, and let rest for 15 minutes before serving.

VARIATION:
May add spinach, carrots, and red and green bell peppers, if desired. Grate (or process in a food processor) whichever vegetables you like, and add up to 1 cup to the meatloaf.

Meatballs Made Easy

Baking makes this process so much easier. The meatballs cook so much more evenly, and as long as you cook them in a nice hot oven, the outsides get a nice sear, too.

1 small onion, grated

1 egg

1 teaspoon Worcestershire

¼ cup grated Parmesan cheese

1 tablespoon dried parsley

¾ teaspoon salt

1 teaspoon pepper

¾ teaspoon garlic powder

1⅓ pounds ground beef

⅓ cup bread crumbs

In a medium bowl, combine onion, egg, Worcestershire, Parmesan cheese, parsley, salt, pepper, and garlic powder; mix well. Crumble ground beef into mixture, and mix with your hands until just combined, taking care not to overwork the meat (don't "squeeze" it through your fingers). Add bread crumbs, and mix just until combined.

Now comes the easy part. Turn mixture out onto a cutting board or clean counter, and shape into a rectangle. Pat her down good, and keep working on it until it's perfectly shaped. Using a sharp knife, cut the mixture into 24 squares, or less if you like bigger meatballs. (Now your work is halfway done, because you don't have to eyeball the amounts to make uniform-sized meatballs.)

Roll each square into a ball. Line a baking sheet with aluminum foil (for easy cleanup), and spray with cooking spray. Place meatballs onto baking sheet, and bake at 400° for 18–20 minutes.

VARIATION:
To make Italian Meatballs, use ¼ cup grated Parmesan cheese, 1 tablespoon Italian seasoning in place of parsley, and ⅓ cup Italian bread crumbs rather than plain.

Unstuffed Cabbage Roll Skillet

I had cabbage rolls on the brain when the wheels started turning. . . . What if I cooked all the ingredients together in a skillet and made sort of a deconstructed cabbage roll dish!? Like a casserole. But quicker! Kinda like an "unstuffed" cabbage roll! I grabbed up all the ingredients, and prayed it would work. And it totally did!

1 pound ground beef

1 small cabbage, chopped

1 small onion, diced

1 clove garlic, minced

1 teaspoon salt

1 teaspoon pepper

1 (14.5-ounce) can beef broth (about 1⅔ cups)

1 cup uncooked white rice

TANGY TOMATO TOPPING:

1 (10¾-ounce) can condensed tomato soup

1 teaspoon white vinegar

1 tablespoon brown sugar

Brown ground beef in a large skillet (with tight-fitting lid to ensure the rice cooks properly) over medium-high heat. Add cabbage, onion, garlic, salt, and pepper; continue cooking until cabbage is slightly tender. Add beef broth and rice; stir well. Cover skillet with fitted lid, and reduce heat to medium low. Continue cooking, stirring occasionally, 20–25 minutes or until rice is cooked through. Remove skillet from heat and let rest, covered, for 10 minutes. Serve with Tangy Tomato Topping.

Combine all Tasty Tomato Topping ingredients in small saucepan till heated through; serve with cabbage mixture.

Cheeseburger Pie

This is really good. It's kinda like a quiche and kinda like a breakfast casserole. As a matter of fact, I think I'm totally going to use sausage in this someday and call it just that!

1 pound ground beef

1 medium onion, chopped

½ cup all-purpose flour

1 cup milk

½ teaspoon dry mustard

½ teaspoon black pepper

⅛ teaspoon salt

2 eggs, slightly beaten

1 (1-ounce) packet Onion or Beefy Onion soup mix (such as Lipton's)

8 ounces sharp Cheddar cheese, shredded

Cook ground beef and onion over medium-high heat until meat is browned and cooked through. Drain; set aside. Add flour to a medium bowl. Slowly pour milk into flour, and whisk to combine (if you add the flour to the milk, the flour will clump). Whisk in dry mustard, pepper, salt, and eggs. Mix onion soup mix into meat mixture, then add ½ of cheese; stir to combine.

Spray a 9-inch pie plate with cooking spray; spoon meat mixture into pie plate. Top pie with remaining cheese. Slowly pour milk mixture evenly over pie. Bake at 375° for 30–40 minutes, or until pie is golden brown and bubbly. Remove pie from oven, then let rest for 10 minutes before serving.

VARIATION:
Garnish the pie with dill pickle slices or fresh tomato slices before baking.

Cheeseburger Sliders for a Crowd

From equal parts tight budget and tight schedule have emerged several dishes that we serve quite regularly on weeknights. This is definitely one of them. This recipe makes a monster batch, which is awesome because you can eat half, then freeze the leftovers in pairs, wrapped in freezer paper, and easily reheat in the microwave for little snackers.

1 medium onion, finely diced

2½ pounds lean ground beef

1 teaspoon salt

1 teaspoon black pepper

1 teaspoon garlic powder

12 American cheese slices

24 soft dinner rolls

Condiments of choice

Dice onion, and scatter evenly on a 13x18-inch baking sheet (or 2 standard-size cookie sheets). Spread ground beef evenly on top of onions, pressing down firmly until the meat reaches the edges of the pan and is evenly distributed (a rolling pin works beautifully for this). Season with salt, pepper, and garlic powder. Bake at 400° for 15–17 minutes. Thoroughly drain pan drippings from meat (once halfway through cooking, and then again when meat is done). Immediately top with American cheese slices.

Using a serrated knife, slice rolls in half, then broil (cut side up) in the oven until toasted. Cut burgers into 24 squares. Place 1 burger square into each roll, and serve with traditional condiments. I like mine best with dill pickle slices, ketchup, and mustard.

NOTE:
You can easily cut this recipe in half. I usually don't because I like to freeze the leftovers. Plus the rolls come in packs of 24, and that just seems like slider destiny.

Game Night Sliders

These are perfect for our family game nights! They're fun, the kids can serve themselves, and oh, yeah, they're ooey-gooey, mind-blowingly, cheezily delicious!

1 pound ground beef

1 pound bulk pork sausage

1 pound Velveeta

½ teaspoon onion powder

½ teaspoon black pepper

24 slider buns or soft dinner rolls, toasted or steamed

Brown ground beef and sausage until cooked through. Thoroughly drain pan drippings from meat (once halfway through cooking, and then again when meat is done).

Combine browned meat, Velveeta, onion powder, and black pepper in a saucepan, and heat on low until cheese is melted and bubbly. Serve on slider buns.

Tavern Sandwich

I'll warn you, you'll make a big ol' mess eating these. But it's part of the fun, I think!

2 pounds ground beef

1 large onion, diced

1 teaspoon each: salt, granulated garlic, mustard powder, and paprika

2 teaspoons black pepper

2 teaspoons Worcestershire

1 (10.5-ounce) can beef consommé

12 hamburger buns, toasted

Condiments of choice

In a large skillet, brown ground beef and onion over medium-high heat until beef is cooked through. Drain fat. Add ground beef mixture and remaining ingredients (except buns) to a large pot. Bring mixture to a simmer, then reduce heat, and cook on low, covered, for 4 hours.

To serve, scoop meat with a slotted spoon to allow excess broth to drain off, and serve on a toasted bun. Serve with dill pickle chips, cheese, yellow mustard, or other condiments of choice.

Sweet Chili-Glazed Smoked Pork Chops

Smoked meats are a huge time-saver and hit my weekday lineup at least once a week. Most are already cooked, so they take no time to get on the table, which works wonders with our "crazy, hectic, homework, practice, lions and tigers and bears, oh my!" weeknight routine.

5–6 smoked pork chops (or 1 ham steak)

Juice from 1 medium orange (about 3 tablespoons)

2 tablespoons brown sugar

1 tablespoon chili powder

½ teaspoon granulated garlic

½ teaspoon mustard powder

Line a baking pan with aluminum foil (for easy cleanup), and spray foil with cooking spray. Arrange pork chops in a single layer in pan. (If using a ham steak, blot off any excess liquid with paper towels before applying glaze.)

Combine remaining ingredients in a small bowl, and mix well. Coat top side of pork chops with glaze; discard any excess. Bake at 400° for 20–25 minutes, or until chops are heated through and glaze is caramelized. Baste again with any residual glaze from the pan, if desired. Smoked pork chops and ham steaks are already fully cooked—we're just bringing these to temperature.

NOTE:
Use whichever citrus you have on hand (lemon, grapefruit, etc.), or use prepared fruit juice.

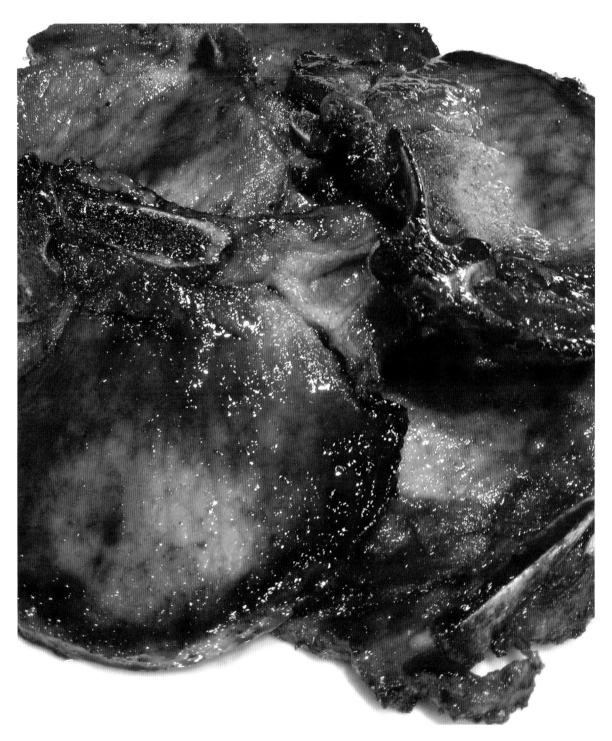

Sweet Chili-Glazed Smoked Pork Chops

Country Fried Pork Chops and Gravy

I know it seems odd to use only salt and pepper, but when it comes to these old-school country recipes, I really just like to stick to the basics. I seriously doubt Nanny was throwing around the garlic or oregano back in her day when frying up pork chops.

Vegetable oil

1½ cups flour (all-purpose or self-rising)

6–8 bone-in pork chops

Salt and pepper to taste

3–4 cups water, divided

Pour enough vegetable oil in a large frying pan to coat the bottom (about ⅛ of an inch deep).

Heat oil on medium-high heat until hot. Add flour to a pie plate or other deep-sided dish; set aside. Season pork chops liberally with salt and pepper, then dredge in flour. Shake off excess flour. Set flour aside.

Cook chops in batches (you don't want to overcrowd the pan) in hot oil until golden brown on each side. Do not flip the chops before they have browned, or some of the breading may stick to the pan. Once all the chops have been cooked, set aside, and keep warm until ready to serve.

Pour off all but ¼ cup of pan drippings, leaving all the bits of goodness in the pan. Add ¼ cup of the remaining flour used to coat the chops to the hot oil. Whisk the flour and oil together, and cook over medium-high heat for 3–4 minutes, or until medium brown. Add 3 cups water to roux, and whisk constantly until smooth and well combined. Reduce heat to medium low, add salt and pepper to taste, and cook for 1–2 minutes. Add more water, until gravy is of desired consistency. Serve with white rice or mashed potatoes.

Smothered Pork Chops

4–6 pork chops

Salt and pepper to taste

½ teaspoon granulated garlic

½ teaspoon dried oregano

3 tablespoons vegetable oil

1 large onion, halved then sliced (like onion rings cut in half)

3 tablespoons all-purpose flour

1 (14-ounce) can chicken broth

Season both sides of pork chops with salt, pepper, garlic, and oregano. Heat oil in a skillet on medium-high heat until hot. Sear pork chops in hot pan for approximately 3 minutes on each side, or until nicely browned. Remove pork chops from pan (we're just searing them).

Add onion to hot pan, season with salt and pepper, and sauté for 2 minutes. Reduce heat to medium, then add flour to onion. Stir to coat onions with flour; continue cooking 2–3 more minutes, stirring occasionally. Slowly add chicken broth; stir until smooth and mixture begins to thicken. Taste for seasoning, then add salt and pepper, if necessary. Reduce heat to low, add pork chops back to pan, then cover and cook 30–60 minutes (you want to see a slight simmer—bump the heat up a notch if you need to, but don't let them boil). The longer they cook, the more tender they are. Serve gravy over pork chops.

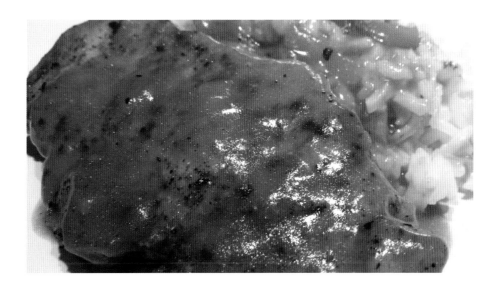

Honey Dijon Pork Kebabs

2 pounds country ribs

¼ cup honey

3 tablespoons Dijon mustard

½ cup soy sauce

3 cloves garlic, minced

2 tablespoons balsamic vinegar

Black pepper to taste

Cut ribs into 2-inch pieces, and place in large zip-top bag. Whisk together honey, Dijon, soy sauce, garlic, and vinegar until thoroughly combined. Reserve ⅓ cup marinade, and set aside. Pour the remaining marinade over the pork. Seal zip-top bag, refrigerate, and marinate 6–8 hours.

Place pork on skewers; sprinkle with black pepper. Grill low and slow, about 30 minutes over low heat; baste with reserved marinade until done.

NOTE:
If you can't find country ribs (which are just a thick boneless pork rib), buy a small Boston butt roast, and cut into 2-inch pieces.

Pan-Seared Pork Medallions and Perfect Pork Marinade

PORK:

1 (1½-pound) pork tenderloin

3 tablespoons vegetable oil

Salt and pepper to taste

MARINADE:

½ cup soy sauce

3 tablespoons vegetable oil

3 tablespoons brown sugar

3 cloves garlic, smashed

1 teaspoon chili powder

1 teaspoon paprika

Place pork tenderloin in a large zip-top plastic bag; set aside. In a small bowl, whisk Marinade ingredients until thoroughly combined. Add Marinade to the pork tenderloin, and seal bag tightly. Marinate pork for 6–8 hours, or overnight.

Remove tenderloin from Marinade, and slice into 8 (2-inch-thick) medallions. Discard marinade. Season each medallion lightly with salt and pepper. Add 3 tablespoons vegetable oil to a large skillet over medium-high heat. Add medallions, and sear for 3–4 minutes or until nicely browned. Flip medallions, reduce heat to medium, and cover skillet. Cook, covered, for 5–6 minutes or until medallions are just done. Remove from heat, and rest for 5 minutes before serving.

Slow Cooker Pulled Pork with Buzzy's Butt Rub

I don't know why I decided to name this rub after my husband's pet name for me. Maybe because it sounds fun and silly and not (ever) too serious . . . and, well, that's how I like things.

BUZZY'S BUTT RUB:

1½ teaspoons salt

½ teaspoon black pepper

½ teaspoon oregano

½ teaspoon granulated garlic

½ teaspoon onion powder

½ teaspoon paprika

¼ teaspoon cayenne pepper

PORK:

1 (6- to 7-pound) Boston butt
   or pork shoulder roast

1 batch Buzzy's Butt Rub

3–4 drops liquid smoke
   (optional)

Barbeque sauce of choice
   (optional)

Add all rub ingredients to a small bowl, and stir until combined. Set aside.

Rinse roast with cold water, then pat dry with paper towels. Rub roast with Buzzy's Butt Rub until evenly coated (don't bother applying the rub to the bottom of the roast if it still has the fatty layer—you're not going to eat that fat, so why waste your seasoning on it, right?). Cover rubbed roast with plastic wrap and refrigerate overnight, if possible. (It's not a deal-breaker if you can't, but it's SO much better if it can soak up the flavors of the rub overnight.)

Place the roast, fat-side down (if applicable), in a large slow cooker. Cover, and cook on HIGH for 4 hours. Add liquid smoke, if desired (not directly onto the roast), then reduce heat to LOW, and continue cooking for 4 more hours. Turn off heat, and let "rest," covered for 30–45 minutes.

Shred or cut the sections of meat as preferred. Toss, or serve with barbeque sauce, if desired.

Coca-Cola Glazed Ham with Brown Sugar and Dijon

I like to make ham two different ways. I either bake it in a baking bag with a can of Coca-Cola (because it's wicked easy and bastes itself), or I make a glaze with Dijon mustard, brown sugar, and orange juice. When I asked on my Facebook page which recipe they would rather have, it was almost a dead tie. So, I decided to combine the two methods and see what happened. I got the best of both worlds . . . .

1 (10- to 12-pound) bone-in cured ham (not spiral)

1 extra large (or "turkey size") oven bag

½ cup brown sugar

⅓ cup Dijon mustard

1 large orange, washed and cut into 6 wedges (optional)

1 (12-ounce) can Coca-Cola

NOTE:
If using a 13- to 15-pound ham, cook 2½–3 hours.

Using a sharp knife, score the ham in a diamond pattern, making ¼-inch deep slices. Place the ham (on its side—not face down) in the oven bag; place in a large roasting pan. Roll the sides of the bag down so that the bag is open wide, and you can get your hands around the ham easily.

Combine brown sugar and Dijon mustard in a small bowl, and stir until thoroughly combined. Rub sugar mixture all over ham. Place orange wedges around the bottom of the ham. Pour Coca-Cola into the bag around the bottom of the ham (not over it). "Puff up" the bag a little by gathering air or blowing into the bag so that the bag isn't touching the ham. Making sure to keep a "loose fit" around the ham, close the bag tightly with the provided tie. Using a small, sharp knife, make 3 small slits in top of bag for ventilation. (Don't skip this step or the bag will burst.)

Move your oven rack low enough so the bag won't touch the upper elements in your oven; bake at 350° for 2–2½ hours or until nicely browned and caramelized. Remove ham from oven, and let rest inside the bag for 30 minutes before serving.

Sweet and Tangy Smoked Sausage

I think maybe a lot of you are just like me . . . you're crazy busy, and working with a limited budget, but you still want to sit down with your family every night and eat supper. We have this at least twice a month. I usually serve this with boiled potatoes and pork n' beans. Just good ol' blue collar grub made with good ol' working mama love. Enjoy!

1 pound smoked sausage

2 tablespoons yellow mustard

2 tablespoons brown sugar

Cut smoked sausage evenly into 6–8 pieces. Slice each piece in half, lengthwise, stopping just short of cutting all the way through, so it opens each piece like a little book. Arrange sausage pieces on a baking sheet, cut-side up (skin down). Broil sausage in the oven until sizzling and starting to brown. Remove sausage from oven, and baste with mixture of mustard and brown sugar. Return sausage to oven, and continue broiling until browned and bubbly. (Watch it closely! You don't want these babies to burn.)

Cakes

What I love about Earthquake Cake is that you end up with a moist, delicious cake you don't have to frost because the ooey-gooey cream cheese mixture becomes an internal frosting explosion that cracks the cake apart with its awesomeness. Hence the name, y'all.

Honey Bun Cake

¾ cup packed brown sugar

1 teaspoon cinnamon

⅓ cup chopped pecans (optional)

⅔ cup vegetable oil

4 eggs

1 cup sour cream

1 box yellow cake mix

Dash of nutmeg

1 cup powdered sugar

4 teaspoons water

1 teaspoon vanilla extract

NOTE:

There are two basic types of honey buns. Those with thin white icing, and those with a glazed icing. Since I like the glazed ones better, and because I leave this cake out at room temperature, I used water instead of milk for my glaze. If you like the white icing better, simply use milk instead of water, and store leftovers in refrigerator, if you have any, which I sincerely doubt!

Combine brown sugar, cinnamon, and pecans, if desired; set aside. Spray a 9x13-inch baking pan with cooking spray; set aside. Mix oil, eggs, and sour cream in medium bowl with electric mixer until well combined. Add cake mix and nutmeg; mix at medium-low speed for 2 minutes.

Pour half of cake batter into baking pan. Sprinkle brown sugar mixture evenly over cake batter. Pour remaining cake batter over top; spread evenly. Bake at 350° for 30–35 minutes or until toothpick inserted in the center comes out clean.

Combine powdered sugar, water, and vanilla, and whisk together until smooth. If icing is too thick, add more water, 1 teaspoon at a time, until thin enough to spread. Spread icing evenly over top of warm cake. Once cool, cover, and store cake at room temperature.

Italian Bakeless Cake

I can't begin to tell you how wonderful this recipe is! It's a lot like banana pudding in that there are vanilla wafers that soak up a pudding-like mixture. Oh . . . my . . . goodness, it's yummy!

1 (14-ounce) can sweetened condensed milk

¼ cup fresh lemon juice

1 (8-ounce) can crushed pineapple, undrained

40–50 vanilla wafers, divided

1 (8-ounce) carton Cool Whip, thawed

2 cups sweetened flaked coconut

12–16 maraschino cherries, rinsed

Whisk together sweetened condensed milk and lemon juice in a small bowl until thoroughly combined. Mix in pineapple (with juice), and set aside. Cover bottom of 8x8-inch glass baking dish with 20–25 vanilla wafers. Pour the pineapple mixture evenly over vanilla wafers, then add remaining vanilla wafers on top. Spread Cool Whip evenly on top of vanilla wafers, then sprinkle with coconut. Top with cherries, then cover and refrigerate at least 8 hours before serving.

Strawberries and Cream Cake

1 box white cake mix

Egg whites, oil, and water per cake mix instructions

1 (8-ounce) package cream cheese, at room temperature

¼ cup milk

½ cup powdered sugar

1 (8-ounce) tub Cool Whip, thawed

3 cups sliced fresh strawberries

1 (12-ounce) container strawberry glaze

Prepare and bake cake mix per package instructions for a 9x13-inch cake. Cool cake completely. Beat cream cheese, milk, and powdered sugar with an electric mixer until fluffy and smooth. Add Cool Whip; stir until combined. Spread cream cheese mixture evenly over cooled cake. Combine strawberry slices and strawberry glaze, and gently stir until strawberries are coated with glaze. Spread strawberries over cream cheese mixture, and refrigerate until ready to serve. Store in refrigerator.

NOTE:
Strawberry glaze can be found in the produce section.

Chocolate Butterfinger Cake

1 box chocolate cake mix

Eggs, oil, and water per cake mix instructions

1 cup caramel ice cream syrup

1 can vanilla cake frosting

16 snack-size Butterfinger candy bars, chopped

Prepare cake mix per instructions for 2 (8- or 9-inch) round cake pans. Cool in pans. Place 1 layer, top-side up, on a serving plate. Pierce cake 10–12 times with fork. Drizzle half the caramel syrup over cake. (Most of it will be absorbed by the cake, but it's okay if some of it drips over the side.) Top with half the frosting, and sprinkle with half the chopped candy bars. Place the second layer on top of the first (top-side up), and repeat the same steps with the remaining caramel syrup, frosting, and chopped candy bars. Store at room temperature in an airtight container.

Preacher Cake

The way I heard it told, Preacher Cake got its name because it was a cake you usually had the ingredients for in your pantry, so if the preacher told you he was coming to visit, you could whip one up with what you had on hand.

CAKE:

3 cups all-purpose flour

2 teaspoons baking soda

1 teaspoon salt

½ teaspoon cinnamon

2 cups sugar

3 eggs

1 cup vegetable oil

2 teaspoons vanilla extract

1 (20-ounce) can crushed pineapple, with juice

1½ cups finely chopped pecans or walnuts, divided

1 cup flaked coconut (optional)

CREAM CHEESE FROSTING:

1 (8-ounce) package cream cheese, at room temperature

½ cup (1 stick) butter, at room temperature

1 teaspoon vanilla extract

2 cups powdered sugar, sifted

Sift together flour, baking soda, salt, and cinnamon; set aside. Combine sugar, eggs, oil, and vanilla; mix on medium-low speed with an electric mixer until creamy. Slowly add flour mixture until just combined. Add pineapple (with juice), 1 cup chopped pecans, and coconut, if desired, and mix on medium-low speed until thoroughly combined (about 1 minute).

Spray a 9x13-inch baking pan with cooking spray. Pour cake batter into pan, and bake at 350° for 45–50 minutes, or until toothpick inserted in center of cake comes out clean. Cool cake completely in pan, then frost with Cream Cheese Frosting. Sprinkle remaining ½ cup chopped pecans over cake. Store in refrigerator.

Whip cream cheese, butter, and vanilla with an electric mixer until fluffy (about 2 minutes). Beat in powdered sugar; add more, if necessary, to reach desired consistency. Makes enough to frost a 9x13-inch cake; double recipe, if making a layered cake.

Mandarin Orange Cake

I think this recipe hit the scene in the 80s, and is known by a few other names: Pig Pickin' Cake, Ambrosia Cake, Pea Picking Cake, Sunshine Cake. . . . My family calls it Mama's Man Cake since Mom says she has yet to serve this to a man who has not asked for it again and again.

CAKE:

½ cup vegetable oil

4 eggs

2 (11-ounce) can mandarin oranges, divided

1 box yellow cake mix

FROSTING:

1 (20-ounce) can crushed pineapple, with juice

1 (5.1-ounce) box vanilla instant pudding mix

1 (16-ounce) carton frozen whipped topping, thawed

Grease and flour 3 round cake pans; set aside. Using electric mixer, beat oil, eggs, and 1 can oranges (with juice) on medium speed until thoroughly combined. Add cake mix, and beat on low speed for 2 minutes. Pour evenly into cake pans, and bake per package instructions for 3 layers. Cool completely, then frost. Garnish with remaining can (drained) mandarin oranges. Refrigerate until ready to serve. Store in refrigerator.

Gently fold Frosting ingredients until thoroughly combined.

Fresh Apple Cake with Butter Pecan Glaze

CAKE:

3 cups all-purpose flour

2 teaspoons cinnamon

1 teaspoon baking soda

¾ teaspoon salt

2 cups firmly packed brown sugar

1¼ cups vegetable oil

½ cup applesauce

3 eggs

4 cups grated apples

1 cup chopped pecans

2 teaspoons vanilla extract

BUTTER PECAN GLAZE:

¾ cup pecan halves

¼ cup butter

¾ cup firmly packed brown sugar

¼ cup heavy cream

¼ cup corn syrup

½ teaspoon vanilla extract

Grease and flour a 10-inch fluted tube pan. Combine flour, cinnamon, baking soda, and salt in medium bowl. In separate bowl, beat brown sugar, oil, applesauce, and eggs with an electric mixer. Gradually add flour mixture. Stir in apples, pecans, and vanilla. Pour into prepared pan.

Bake at 350° for 50–55 minutes or until toothpick inserted in center comes out clean. Cool cake 15 minutes in pan, then remove and set on a cake plate in its upright position. Cool completely.

Sauté pecans in butter over medium heat for 2 minutes, stirring constantly. Mix in brown sugar, cream, and corn syrup. Bring to a rolling boil. Cook about 2 minutes, stirring constantly. Remove from heat. Stir in vanilla extract. Cool until thickened. Drizzle over cake. Extra glaze may be spooned over individual slices, if desired.

VARIATIONS:

Fresh Pear Cake: Substitute the grated apples with grated pears. Keep the applesauce or substitute with pear sauce (found with the individual applesauce packages for kids).

Fresh Peach Cake: Substitute grated apples and applesauce with 4½ cups finely chopped fresh peaches.

Bananas Foster Cake: Substitute grated apples and applesauce with 4½ cups mashed bananas.

Raspberry Zinger Poke Cake

If you have no idea what a Raspberry Zinger is, it's a snack cake made by Hostess. It's a little baby cream-filled white cake coated with raspberry goodness rolled in coconut. And this cake tastes just like one—only better!

1 box white cake mix

Egg whites, water, and oil per cake mix instructions

1 (4-serving) box raspberry-flavored gelatin

⅔ cup boiling water

⅔ cup ice water

1 (8-ounce) tub Cool Whip

2–3 cups sweetened flaked coconut

Bake cake per package instructions for a 9x13-inch pan. Cool cake completely in the pan. Poke holes in cake, using a serving fork, skewer, or whatever gets it done (try not to use a regular fork if the tines are pretty close together, because it might tear up the cake too much).

Mix gelatin with boiling water; stir until completely dissolved. Stir in ice water, then slowly pour gelatin mixture evenly over cake. Cover cake, and refrigerate until cool. Ice cake with Cool Whip, then sprinkle evenly with coconut. Cover, and refrigerate until ready to serve.

Chocolate Peanut Butter Poke Cake

I will definitely be making this to bring to the next family function or potluck, because it's so easy to make and so beautiful and so delicious!

1 box chocolate cake mix

Eggs, water, and oil per cake mix instructions

1 (8-ounce) block cream cheese, at room temperature

1 (14-ounce) can sweetened condensed milk

1 cup creamy peanut butter

1 (12-ounce) tub Cool Whip, divided

Chocolate sauce (such as Hershey's)

3 tablespoons chopped peanuts (optional)

Bake cake per package instructions for 9x13-inch cake. Cool cake completely. Using handle of a standard-size wooden spoon, poke 30–35 holes in cake (do not use a fork—the holes have to be big enough for the thick peanut butter pie filling).

Combine cream cheese and condensed milk in a large bowl or stand mixer, and beat until smooth. Add peanut butter, mixing until thoroughly incorporated. Add half of Cool Whip (about 3 cups), mixing until well combined and smooth. (You'd typically be told to "gently fold" Cool Whip into a recipe like this, but here you're going to want to really mix it—the longer you mix it, the thinner it will become, and you need it to thin out a little to spread and fill the holes.) Spread peanut butter mixture evenly over cake. Cover, and refrigerate at least 6 hours.

To serve, spread remaining Cool Whip over peanut butter mixture. Drizzle chocolate sauce over top, then sprinkle with chopped peanuts. Store in refrigerator.

German Chocolate Sheet Cake

I decided to use a regular chocolate cake mix instead of German chocolate, because I get the impression the latter gets its lighter color because it has less cocoa in it. To get the traditional lighter color, I just added a little sour cream. That way we get all the chocolate plus a little added richness.

CAKE:

1 box chocolate cake mix

Eggs, oil, and water per cake mix instructions

½ cup sour cream (optional)

FROSTING:

1 (12-ounce) can evaporated milk

1 cup (2 sticks) butter

1½ cups sugar

¼ teaspoon salt

1 teaspoon vanilla

2 cups sweetened flaked coconut

1¼ cups chopped pecans

Spray a 9x13-inch baking pan with cooking spray; set aside. Prepare cake batter per package instructions, then stir in sour cream, if desired. Bake per instructions for a 9x13-inch cake. Remove cake from oven, and allow to cool while preparing Frosting.

Heat evaporated milk, butter, sugar, and salt in a medium saucepan over medium heat until boiling, stirring frequently. Reduce heat to medium low, and simmer 12–15 minutes, or until a light caramel color, stirring occasionally. Remove from heat; stir in vanilla, coconut, and pecans. Let icing cool 5 minutes, then spread over cooled cake. Let cake rest, uncovered, 2 hours before serving. Store, covered, at room temperature—cake does not need to be refrigerated.

German Chocolate Sheet Cake

Earthquake Cake

What I love about this is that you end up with a moist, delicious cake you don't have to frost because the ooey-gooey cream cheese mixture becomes an internal frosting explosion that cracks the cake apart with its awesomeness. Hence the name, y'all.

1 cup chopped pecans

2 cups sweetened flaked coconut

1 box chocolate cake mix

Eggs, oil, and water per cake mix instructions

½ cup butter, melted

1 (8-ounce) package cream cheese, at room temperature

3 cups powdered sugar

1 cup semisweet chocolate chips

Spray a 9x13-inch pan with cooking spray. Scatter pecans and coconut evenly into pan. Prepare cake batter per package instructions, and pour over pecans and coconut. Combine melted butter and cream cheese in a medium bowl; beat with an electric mixer until smooth. Add powdered sugar, 1 cup at a time; beat on low until smooth and creamy. Dollop heaping tablespoons of cream cheese mixture evenly onto cake batter. Sprinkle cake with chocolate chips. Bake at 350° for 40–45 minutes or until set.

NOTE:
Some folks have reported their cakes overflowed while cooking. I have never had this even come close to happening, but you may want to set your pan on a larger baking sheet just in case.

Chocolate Mint Cream Cake

FILLING:

8 ounces cream cheese, softened

¼ cup sugar

2 tablespoons butter, softened

1 tablespoon cornstarch

1 egg

2 tablespoons milk

¾ teaspoon peppermint extract

BATTER:

1 chocolate cake mix

1 cup water

⅓ cup vegetable oil

3 eggs

GLAZE:

⅓ cup light corn syrup

⅓ cup whipping cream

6 ounces semisweet baking chocolate, chopped

DRIZZLE:

2 ounces white baking chocolate, chopped

1 teaspoon vegetable oil

¼ teaspoon peppermint extract

Combine Filling ingredients, and beat with mixer until smooth; set aside.

Combine Batter ingredients, and mix according to package instructions. Spread 2 cups Batter into greased and floured Bundt pan. Spread Filling on top. Pour in remaining Batter. Bake at 325° for 50–55 minutes, or until cake tester comes out clean. Cool 10 minutes in pan, then cool completely on cooling rack or serving plate.

For the Glaze, bring corn syrup and whipping cream to a simmer over medium heat, stirring constantly. Add semisweet chocolate; stir until smooth. Pour Glaze over cake. Refrigerate 15–20 minutes before adding Drizzle.

For Drizzle, microwave, then stir, white chocolate and oil at 30-second intervals until smooth and melted. Stir in extract. Drizzle over cake. Refrigerate 15–20 minutes. Store at room temperature until ready to serve.

VARIATION:

Instead of using Glaze and Drizzle, combine ¾ can chocolate frosting and ¼ teaspoon peppermint extract in a microwave-safe bowl; stir well. Microwave, then stir, at 20-second intervals until frosting is thin enough to drizzle over cake. Drizzle frosting over cake. Refrigerate for 15–20 minutes. Remove cake from refrigerator, and store at room temperature until ready to serve.

Oreo Crunch Chocolate Ice Cream Cake

1 (1.75-quart) container chocolate ice cream (no substitutions)

1 (14.3-ounce) package Oreo cookies (36 cookies)

2 (7.25-ounce) bottles Magic Shell chocolate-flavored topping

1 (8-ounce) tub frozen Cool Whip, thawed

Set ice cream out at room temperature for about 30 minutes to soften. (You want to be able to slide a butter knife into it without too much resistance.)

Meanwhile, crush cookies in a large bowl. Shake Magic Shell and pour both containers into bowl with crushed cookies; stir well. Close Magic Shell containers tight, then turn upside-down; set aside. (There's still a good bit left in the containers that you'll use later to drizzle on top of the cake.) Spread half (or a little more) of cookie mixture evenly over bottom of 9x13-inch baking pan to cover it completely. Place pan in freezer for cookie layer to firm up.

In large bowl, mix ice cream and Cool Whip just until thoroughly combined. Remove pan from freezer, then spread ice cream mixture evenly over cookie layer. Sprinkle top of ice cream layer evenly with remaining cookie mixture. Drizzle remaining Magic Shell evenly over top. Cover, and freeze 6–8 hours before serving.

Oreo Crunch Chocolate Ice Cream Cake

Fried Ice Cream Cake

1 (1.75-quart) container
vanilla ice cream (no
substitutions)

½ cup butter (1 stick)

1 cup sugar

½ teaspoon salt

3 cups crushed cornflakes

1 (8-ounce) tub Cool Whip,
thawed

¾ teaspoon cinnamon

Honey for drizzling

Set ice cream out at room temperature for about 30 minutes to soften. You want to be able to slide a butter knife into it without too much resistance.

Meanwhile, melt butter in a large skillet over medium-high heat; add sugar and salt. Stir, and cook until sugar is thoroughly incorporated and mixture starts to bubble (2–3 minutes). Add cornflakes, and cook, stirring constantly, 5–6 minutes or until cornflakes are slightly caramelized and browned. (Be careful not to cook too long, or the sugar will burn.)

Add a little more than half of cornflakes to bottom of 9x13-inch baking dish. Using your hand, pat the cornflakes into a level crust in bottom of dish. Let crust cool to room temperature.

In large bowl, mix ice cream, Cool Whip, and cinnamon just until thoroughly combined. Spread ice cream mixture evenly over cornflake layer. Sprinkle top of ice cream evenly with remaining cornflakes. Cover, and freeze "cake" for 4 hours before serving. Drizzle each portion with honey before serving.

NOTE:
I was able to serve and enjoy this straight out of the freezer. But, if your freezer is set on some subarctic dinosaur preserving setting, you may want to let this sit in the fridge for an hour or so to soften up before serving.

Peanut Butter Brownie Cheesecake

1 box brownie mix

¾ cup hot fudge topping, warmed

2 (8-ounce) packages cream cheese, softened

1½ cups crunchy peanut butter

1 (14-ounce) can sweetened condensed milk

1 (12-ounce) tub frozen whipped topping, thawed

1½ cups chopped mini peanut butter cups

2 tablespoons chocolate syrup

Prepare brownie mix according to package instructions, using a 9x13-inch pan. Cool completely; set aside. Cut brownies into small chunks. Using ⅔ of the brownie chunks, press brownies into bottom of a 9-inch springform pan, forming an even crust. Spread with warm fudge topping; set aside. Crumble remaining brownies, and set aside.

In a large mixing bowl, beat cream cheese and peanut butter with an electric mixer on medium speed until combined. Add condensed milk; beat until just combined. Fold in ⅔ of the whipped topping until thoroughly incorporated.

Spread ½ of cream cheese mixture over brownie crust. Sprinkle with ½ of reserved brownie crumbles. Spread remaining cream cheese mixture over brownies. Top with remaining whipped topping. Sprinkle with remaining brownie crumbles and peanut butter cups. Drizzle with chocolate syrup. Cover, and refrigerate for 6 hours before serving.

The Perfect Cheesecake

CRUST:

2 cups gingersnap crumbs (half of an 18-ounce bag yields 2 cups)

¼ cup sugar

4 tablespoons butter, melted

FILLING:

4 (8-ounce) packages cream cheese, at room temperature

Juice of 1 lemon

2 teaspoons vanilla extract

6 eggs

2¼ cups sugar

2 tablespoons all-purpose flour

1 pint heavy whipping cream

For Crust, combine gingersnap crumbs, sugar, and butter in a medium bowl; mix well. Press mixture into bottom and 1½ inches up side of a 10-inch springform pan.

For Filling, mix cream cheese, lemon juice, and vanilla in a large bowl at medium speed until smooth and creamy. Add eggs, one at a time, beating well after each. Scrape sides of bowl. Add sugar and flour, mixing at low speed for 5 minutes. Add whipping cream, and mix just until Filling is smooth and creamy. Pour into Crust.

Set oven rack to the middle position. Preheat oven to 350°. Bring 4 cups of water to a boil.

Place springform pan on a large piece of foil, and crimp foil around bottom of pan and halfway up the side to create a watertight "shell." Place springform pan into a large baking pan.

Pour enough boiling water into baking pan to come about 1 inch up side of springform pan. Bake 1 hour. Turn oven off; leave cheesecake in oven for 30–45 minutes. Cheesecake is done when it is mostly set and only a small circle in the center jiggles slightly (the center will firm up during the cooling process). Remove from oven, and let cool to room temperature. Once cool, cover, and refrigerate at least 8 hours.

Serve plain or with chocolate sauce, cherry pie filling, lemon curd, fresh fruit, or whatever else suits your fancy. I was fancying some cherries, so that's what I used!

The Perfect Cheesecake

Mandy's Pound Cake

1 cup butter

½ cup shortening

3 cups sugar

1 teaspoon vanilla extract

2 teaspoons butternut or
  lemon extract

5 large eggs

3 cups all-purpose flour

2 teaspoons baking powder

1 teaspoon salt

1¼ cups buttermilk

Allow all ingredients to come to room temperature, especially eggs. Cream butter and shortening in a large mixing bowl or stand mixer. Gradually add sugar and extracts, beating until light and fluffy. Add eggs, one at a time, beating well after each.

Sift together flour, baking powder, and salt in separate bowl. Slowly add flour mixture to creamed mixture, alternating with buttermilk (beginning and ending with flour mixture).

Pour into a greased and floured 10-inch tube pan, and bake at 350° for 1 hour and 15 minutes, or until toothpick inserted in the center comes out clean. Cool in pan, then plate top-side up. Store at room temperature in airtight container.

Cookies & Candies

Every time I open a bag of Bugles I always think, man, I'd love to pump these full of peanut butter and dip them in chocolate, which is more proof that I spend WAY too much time thinking about recipes. So when I saw a display of Bugles at the store, I decided that was exactly what I would do. I should warn you though . . . husbands and children can't keep out of them. These Chocolate-Dipped Peanut Butter Bugles are da bomb!

Dawn's Chocolate Chunk Cookies

¾ cup firmly packed brown sugar

½ cup sugar

1 cup butter, softened

1 egg

1½ teaspoons vanilla

2¼ cups all-purpose flour

1 teaspoon baking soda

½ teaspoon salt

1 (8-ounce) milk chocolate candy bar, cut into ½-inch pieces

1 cup toffee bits

1 cup chopped walnuts (optional)

Combine brown sugar, sugar, butter, egg, and vanilla in a stand mixer fitted with a paddle attachment or a large mixing bowl, and mix on medium speed until well blended.

Combine flour, baking soda, and salt in a separate bowl, and stir to combine. Add flour mixture to sugar mixture; mix until all ingredients are incorporated. Add chocolate pieces, toffee bits, and nuts; stir to combine.

Using a tablespoon, drop rounded spoonfuls of dough onto ungreased cookie sheet; bake at 375° for 9–11 minutes or until bottom edges start to brown.

NOTE:
These cookies are best when cooked on a medium-weight stainless steel baking sheet.

Chewy, Orange-Kissed Sugar Cookies

1 cup butter, at room temperature

1½ cups white sugar

1 egg

Zest of 1 large orange or 2 lemons

1 tablespoon freshly squeezed orange juice, or 2 teaspoons lemon juice

1 teaspoon vanilla extract

2¾ cups all-purpose flour

1 teaspoon baking soda

½ teaspoon baking powder

1 teaspoon salt

Sprinkles or sugar for rolling cookies

NOTE:

I use a 1½-inch cookie scoop to portion out my cookies. I pack the dough in level then pop the dough out and roll the rounded part in the sprinkles (not the flat bottom). The dough pops out dome-shaped, which is perfect because I don't have to try to roll them into balls.

Cream together butter and sugar with an electric mixer set at medium speed until fluffy (about 2 minutes). Add egg, orange zest, orange juice, and vanilla; mix until ingredients are combined and smooth.

Sift together flour, baking soda, baking powder, and salt; slowly add dry ingredients to butter mixture. Mix on low speed until combined. Dough will be thick.

Roll dough into 1½-inch balls, roll in sprinkles, and place on a cookie sheet or baking pan 2 inches apart. Bake at 350° for 10–12 minutes or until cookies just begin to brown on the bottom. Cool cookies on cookie sheet for 5 minutes; then remove to a clean surface to cool completely. Store cookies in an airtight container.

Snowball Cookies

1 cup butter, at room temperature

½ cup powdered sugar

1 teaspoon vanilla extract

Pinch of salt

1¾ cups all-purpose flour

1 cup finely chopped pecans

Additional powdered sugar

Using an electric mixer, cream together butter, powdered sugar, vanilla, and salt until smooth and creamy. Slowly add flour, then pecans, and mix until combined. Roll into 1-inch balls, and bake on an ungreased cookie sheet at 275° for 35–40 minutes or until cookies just start to brown on the bottom.

Remove cookies from oven, and immediately roll in additional powdered sugar. Once cool, store in an airtight container.

NOTE:
As with all of my recipes, use real, salted butter.

Kitchen Sink (No-Bake!) Cookies

I'm always experimenting with this recipe, and this time, I found my favorite. I called these Kitchen Sink Cookies because . . . I put a little bit of everything in these babies! You get it, right? Everything but the kitchen sink? Okay, just had to check!

2 cups sugar

½ cup cocoa

1 stick real butter (½ cup)

⅔ cup milk

1 cup peanut butter

1 teaspoon vanilla

3 cups uncooked oatmeal (old-fashioned or quick-cooking)

1 heaping cup raisins

1 cup chopped almonds and/or peanuts

1 cup sweetened flaked coconut (optional)

Combine sugar, cocoa, butter, and milk in a large saucepan. Bring to a boil over medium-high heat, stirring constantly. Once mixture reaches a boil, continue cooking 1 full minute. Remove from heat immediately.

Add peanut butter and vanilla; stir well. Add oatmeal, raisins, nuts, and coconut, if desired; stir until well combined. Drop mixture by rounded teaspoonfuls (I use a cookie scoop) onto wax paper. Cool several hours until set and firm.

NOTE:
You may use any kind of nut you prefer. If using unsalted nuts, add a pinch of salt when you add the nuts.

No-Bake Peanut Butter Oatmeal Cookies with Chocolate Glaze

2 cups sugar

Dash of salt

1 stick butter (½ cup)

½ cup milk

1 cup peanut butter

1 teaspoon vanilla

3 cups uncooked oats

Cocoa, powdered sugar, and
  water for glaze

In a large saucepan, bring sugar, salt, butter, and milk to a boil over medium heat for 1 full minute. Remove from heat immediately.

Add peanut butter and vanilla; stir well. Add oatmeal, and stir until thoroughly incorporated. On a sheet of wax paper, drop mixture by the teaspoonfuls. To make a glaze, drizzle with a mixture of cocoa, powdered sugar, and water. Cool several hours, until firm.

NOTE:
I prefer quick-cooking oats over old-fashioned in this recipe, but either will work.

Pecan Chewies

1 cup butter (2 sticks), melted

1 cup sugar

1 cup brown sugar

2 eggs

2 teaspoons vanilla extract

2 cups all-purpose flour

1 tablespoon baking powder

1 teaspoon salt

1½ cups roughly chopped pecans

Cream together butter, sugar, brown sugar, eggs, and vanilla with an electric mixer at medium speed until smooth and creamy (about 1 minute).

Sift together flour, baking powder, and salt. Gradually add flour mixture to butter mixture, and mix until just combined and smooth (about 1 minute). Stir in pecans.

Spray a 9x13-inch baking pan with cooking spray. Spread batter evenly into pan, and bake at 300° for 40 minutes or until set in the middle and golden brown.

Cut into squares, and store in an airtight container once cooled.

Fudge-Stuffed Chocolate Chip Cookie Bars

2 (16.5-ounce) rolls
  refrigerated chocolate chip
  cookie dough, divided

1 (14-ounce) can sweetened
  condensed milk

1 (12-ounce) package
  semisweet chocolate chips
  (about 2 cups)

2 tablespoons butter

Pinch of salt

Set cookie dough out at room temperature for about 15 minutes to soften. Spray a 9x13-inch baking pan with cooking spray; set aside. Meanwhile, mix sweetened condensed milk, chocolate chips, butter, and salt in a pan over medium heat until chips are melted and mixture is smooth. Remove from heat, stirring occasionally until ready to use.

Press 1 roll and ⅓ of other roll of chocolate chip cookie dough onto bottom of baking pan. Pour chocolate mixture over cookie dough, and spread evenly. Using your fingers, pinch off small dollops of remaining cookie dough, and drop evenly on top of chocolate mixture. Bake at 350° for 20 minutes or until cookie dough is lightly browned. Cool completely in pan; cut into squares. Store, covered, at room temperature.

NOTE:
Lay a sheet of wax paper over the dough, then press down with hands to make quick work of pressing the cookie dough into baking pan.

VARIATION:
These would be awesome with peanut butter cookie dough, too.

Fudge-Stuffed Chocolate Chip Cookie Bars

Chocolate Peanut Butter Oatmeal Bars

Before I tell you how to make these, look at the picture. Do you see that layer of peanut butter goodness? Do you SEE that?! That, my friends, is where the money's at.

1 cup butter (2 sticks), melted

1 cup brown sugar

½ teaspoon baking soda

1 teaspoon salt

1½ cups all-purpose flour

2¼ cups quick-cooking oats

½ cup creamy peanut butter

1 (14-ounce) can sweetened condensed milk

1 (12-ounce) package semisweet chocolate chips (about 2 cups)

Line a 9x13-inch baking pan with aluminum foil; spray with cooking spray; set aside. In large bowl, mix butter, brown sugar, baking soda, and salt with an electric mixer on low speed until smooth. Add flour and oats; mix until well combined. Reserve 1½ cups oat mixture. Press remaining oat mixture into bottom of prepared pan. Bake at 350° for 10 minutes.

Combine peanut butter and condensed milk; mix until smooth. Carefully spread peanut butter mixture evenly over semi-cooked oat crust, being careful to keep the top of the crust from crumbling into peanut butter mixture. Sprinkle half of reserved oat mixture over peanut butter mixture. Top with chocolate chips; sprinkle remaining oat mixture on top. Bake 25 more minutes or until oat crumbles start to brown. Cool completely in pan, then remove by lifting up on aluminum foil. Cut into bars, and store in an airtight container.

Mud Hen Bars

If you're not a marshmallow person, don't let these throw you off. I'm not a huge marshmallow person myself, but that's one of the cool things about this recipe . . . the marshmallows mostly melt away. And that brown sugar meringue-ish topping takes the shape of them before they melt, which is what gives you all the cool bumps.

BOTTOM LAYER:

1½ cups all-purpose flour

1 teaspoon baking powder

½ teaspoon salt

½ cup butter, at room temperature

1 cup sugar

1 whole egg

2 egg yolks (reserve whites for top layer)

1 teaspoon vanilla

MIDDLE LAYER:

1 cup semisweet chocolate chips

1 cup mini-marshmallows

1 cup chopped nuts

TOP LAYER:

2 egg whites

1 cup brown sugar

Sift flour, baking powder, and salt into a small bowl; stir to combine. Set aside. With electric mixer, combine butter and sugar until creamy. Add whole egg, egg yolks, and vanilla; mix just until smooth. Slowly add flour mixture, and mix until all ingredients are just combined. Grease or butter a 9x13-inch baking pan. Add dough to pan, and spread evenly to cover bottom.

Top the Bottom Layer evenly with chocolate chips, marshmallows, and nuts.

In a cold, clean mixing bowl, beat egg whites on high speed until stiff peaks form. Fold in brown sugar, and stir until smooth and there are no lumps. Spread egg white mixture evenly on top of Middle Layer.

Bake at 350° for 25–30 minutes or until Top Layer is golden brown. Remove from oven, and cool for 20 minutes before serving. Store in an airtight container.

NOTE:
Lay a sheet of wax paper over the dough, then press down with hands to make quick work of pressing the cookie dough into baking pan.

Snickers Fudge Brownies

Y'all! These are SO easy and wicked good. So, the next time you want to totally rock it out, go for these.

1 (18-ounce) family-size box brownie mix

Eggs, oil, and water for the brownies

2 (9-ounce) bags snack-size Snickers

1 (14-ounce) can sweetened condensed milk

1 (12-ounce) bag semisweet chocolate chips

Pinch of salt

Line a 9x13-inch baking pan with aluminum foil, and spray generously with cooking spray. Bake brownies in prepared pan according to package instructions for 9x13-inch pan. Remove brownies from oven, and cool for 10 minutes. Chop Snickers, and sprinkle evenly on top of brownies. Make the fudge by melting sweetened condensed milk, chocolate chips, and salt over medium-low heat, stirring until smooth. Spread fudge evenly over Snickers (to spread evenly, cover with a sheet of wax paper and press with hands). Refrigerate until firm; remove brownies from pan by lifting up aluminum foil lining. Cut to size; then serve. Store at room temperature.

Magic Brownie Bars

The combination of butterscotch, chocolate, and coconut should have its own name. Like the classical French combination of celery, onion, and carrot is called "Mirepoix," or the Cajun blend of celery, onion, and bell pepper is called the "Holy Trinity," I think butterscotch, chocolate, and coconut should have a name like "Magic Mix" or "Fifty Shades of Brown."

1 (18-ounce) family-size box brownie mix

Eggs, oil, and water for the brownies

1 (11-ounce) bag butterscotch morsels

2 cups sweetened flaked coconut

1 cup chopped pecans (optional)

1 (14-ounce) can sweetened condensed milk

Line a 9x13-inch baking pan with aluminum foil; spray generously with cooking spray. Prepare brownie batter per package instructions; spread brownie batter evenly into pan. Sprinkle butterscotch morsels, coconut, and pecans over brownie batter. Drizzle sweetened condensed milk evenly over morsels, etc. Bake at 350° for 35–40 minutes or until milk is lightly caramelized. Remove from oven, and let rest until cool. Remove from pan by lifting up on aluminum foil lining; cut into servings.

Peanut Butter Chocolate Crunchies

Something amazing happened. My husband got excited about these. That's a big deal, y'all. That's a HUGE deal!

5 cups cornflakes

1 cup light corn syrup

¼ cup sugar

¼ teaspoon salt

2 cups creamy peanut butter

½ teaspoon vanilla extract

1 cup chocolate chips

Pour cornflakes into large bowl; set aside. (Do this first, because you need to work quickly once the corn syrup mixture is ready.) Line a 9x13-inch baking dish with wax paper or aluminum foil; set aside.

Heat corn syrup, sugar, and salt in a medium saucepan over medium heat until boiling; boil 1 minute (no longer), until sugar is no longer gritty. Remove from heat; stir in peanut butter and vanilla until smooth. Pour peanut butter mixture over cornflakes, and gently fold until about halfway combined. Add chocolate chips, and gently combine until cornflakes and chocolate chips are evenly distributed (chocolate chips will melt slightly).

Spread mixture into prepared pan, and tamp down a bit (I laid a sheet of wax paper over it, and pressed down with my hands). Once cool, cover, and refrigerate until chocolate is firm. Lifting up on wax paper or aluminum foil, remove giant awesome slab of goodness from pan; cut into bars. Store in an airtight container at room temperature.

Peanut Butter Chocolate Crunchies

Peanut Butter Blotto Brownies

1 (18-ounce) family-size box brownie mix

Eggs, oil, and water for the brownies

1 (12-ounce) bag chocolate chips, divided

1½ cups peanut butter

1 cup chopped roasted peanuts

8 Nutty Bars, chopped

Line a 9x13-inch baking pan with aluminum foil; spray generously with cooking spray. Prepare and cook brownie batter per package instructions for a 9x13-inch pan. Remove brownies from oven, and sprinkle with ½ cup chocolate chips. (They will start to melt a bit, but just leave them be.)

In medium pan, melt peanut butter and remaining chocolate chips over medium-low heat, stirring constantly until melted and smooth. Remove from heat, and stir in chopped peanuts. Sprinkle chopped Nutty Bars evenly over top of brownies. Pour melted chocolate and peanut butter mixture on top of Nutty Bars. Cool for 30 minutes; refrigerate until firm. Remove brownies from pan; cut into servings.

Fluffernutter Squares

½ cup (1 stick) real, salted butter

1 (10-ounce) bag peanut butter morsels (chips)

1 (10-ounce) bag miniature marshmallows

NOTE:

This recipe doubles easily. Just double all ingredients, and use a 9x13-inch pan instead of a square one.

Line an 8x8- or 9x9-inch square pan with wax paper; set aside. In a large pan, melt butter over medium heat. When butter is melted, reduce heat to medium low; add peanut butter morsels. Stir until completely melted and smooth. Remove from heat, and stir in marshmallows. Stir until all marshmallows are evenly coated.

Spread mixture into prepared pan; refrigerate until set, 2–3 hours. Once set, lift from pan by pulling up on wax paper. Cut into 16 squares. Cover, and refrigerate to store.

Mr. Goodbar Clusters

2 cups salted cocktail peanuts

1 (12-ounce) bag semisweet chocolate chips

1 (12-ounce) bag milk chocolate chips

2 tablespoons peanut butter

NOTE:

You don't have to mix the milk chocolate and semisweet chips; you can use one or the other, but I really think the combination nails the Mr. Goodbar taste! If you decide to use all milk chocolate, omit the peanut butter—the milk chocolate is soft enough without it.

Using a large knife, chop peanuts (you just want to quarter a whole peanut, so don't use a nut grinder or texture will be too fine). Set aside. Melt semisweet and milk chocolate chips in microwave until completely melted and smooth. Add peanut butter; stir well. Add chopped peanuts; stir well. Drop by tablespoonfuls onto wax or parchment paper. Let clusters sit until firm, about 9 hours. (You can speed this up by putting them in the refrigerator, but they will sweat a little when you take them out, which will mar up the smooth chocolate finish.)

Chocolate-Dipped Peanut Butter Bugles

Every time I open a bag of Bugles I always think, man, I'd love to pump these full of peanut butter and dip them in chocolate, which is more proof that I spend WAY too much time thinking about recipes. So when I saw a display of Bugles at the store, I decided that was exactly what I would do. I should warn you though . . . husbands and children can't keep out of them. These babies are da bomb!

1 cup peanut butter

¼ cup powdered sugar

1 (7.5-ounce) bag of Bugles

1 (12-ounce) bag chocolate chips

Combine peanut butter and powdered sugar with electric mixer until creamy. Fill a piping bag or plastic zip-top bag with peanut butter mixture (if using zip-top bag, snip a small hole in one corner). Pipe peanut butter mixture into each Bugle until just full. (You won't be able to use all of the Bugles, because some are duds with flat openings, but that's okay, you'll have enough good ones.) Melt chocolate chips, and dip open ends of stuffed Bugles into chocolate. Set each on aluminum foil or parchment paper for several hours, until chocolate is firm again.

Pink Lemonade Cupcake Truffles

1 box lemon cake mix

Eggs and oil for cake mix

Lemonade

1 (16-ounce) container lemon frosting

Pink sugar sprinkles

Make cake per box instructions for a 9x13-inch pan, substituting water with lemonade. Allow cake to cool completely. Trim off thin golden brown top and edges of cake; you can leave the bottom. (This step is optional, but removing the brown top and edges yields a brighter yellow cake ball batter.)

Break cake into pieces, and add to a large mixing bowl or stand mixer. Add frosting, and mix on low speed (use paddle attachment, if using a stand mixer) until thoroughly combined and smooth. Cover, and refrigerate "batter" for 4–6 hours.

Once batter is cold and firm, form into small balls. I used a cookie scoop to ensure each one was uniform in size. Roll each ball in sugar sprinkles. Store in refrigerator.

Pies & Other Desserts

What do you get when you combine fudgy brownies with Kahlúa liqueur and Starbucks coffee? Complete and total awesomeness. And the best part? It's easy! You're going to look like a total rock star when you whip this Mocha Fudge Pie with Kahlúa and Starbucks out. And no one will ever know how ridiculously easy it is to prepare! Holla! Oh, and another plus? This freezes beautifully! The recipe makes two pies . . . one to eat now and one to throw in the freezer to wow your in-laws the next time they decide to show up unannounced.

Flaky Butter Pie Pastry

1¼ cups all-purpose flour

½ teaspoon sugar

½ teaspoon salt

½ cup (1 stick) cold butter, cut into ½-inch pieces

4–5 tablespoons ice water

Combine flour, sugar, and salt in a food processor; pulse once to mix. Add butter; pulse 6–8 times, until mixture resembles coarse meal, with pea-sized pieces of butter. Add ice water, 1 tablespoon at a time, pulsing until mixture just begins to clump together. Turn dough out onto a clean surface, and shape into a disk about 5 inches in diameter. Sprinkle dough with a little flour; wrap in wax paper or plastic wrap. Refrigerate for 1–24 hours.

When ready to prepare, roll dough into a 12-inch circle with a rolling pin on a lightly floured surface. Carefully place pastry into a 9-inch pie plate; trim edges to within ½ inch of edge of pie dish. Shape edges as desired, either by crimping with your fingers or pressing down with a fork. Perforate bottom of pastry by piercing with a fork 4–5 times (to ventilate and keep crust from bubbling up on bottom); fill, and cook as directed.

Classic Pecan Pie

This is the pecan pie that almost never was. And it came out perfect anyway.

3 eggs, beaten

½ cup sugar

3 tablespoons butter, melted

1 cup dark corn syrup

¼ teaspoon salt

1½ teaspoons vanilla

6 ounces pecans, chopped
(about 1½ cups)

1 (9-inch) pie pastry

Mix eggs and sugar with a whisk until smooth. Add butter, corn syrup, salt, and vanilla, and whisk until smooth. Stir in chopped pecans. Pour filling into pie pastry; bake at 350° for 50 minutes, or until center of pie no longer jiggles. (If needed, cover edges of pie crust with foil to keep the crust from browning too much.)

NOTE:
Use the ready-made frozen pie shells or my recipe for Flaky Butter Pie Pastry (see page 204).

Peanut Butter Cream Pie

1 (14-ounce) can sweetened
condensed milk

1 (8-ounce) block cream
cheese, at room temperature

1 cup peanut butter

1 cup powdered sugar

1 (8-ounce) carton Cool Whip,
thawed, divided

2 (9-inch) chocolate pie shells

Combine condensed milk and cream cheese; beat with an electric mixer on medium speed until smooth. Add peanut butter and powdered sugar; mix until blended. Add half of Cool Whip; mix until smooth. Fold in remaining Cool Whip; mix until just combined. Divide mixture evenly into pie shells. Cover, and refrigerate 6 hours before serving. Store in refrigerator.

Whipped Nutella Cream Pie

1 (13-ounce) jar Nutella

1 pint heavy whipping cream, very cold

1 (9-inch) deep-dish pie crust, prepared (or use my recipe for Flaky Butter Pie Pastry on page 204)

NOTE:

You want your whipping cream to be very cold. I place mine in the freezer for about 45 minutes before whipping.

Add Nutella to a stand mixer or large bowl, and whip with whisk beaters on medium speed until very fluffy (about 2 minutes). Slowly add whipping cream; mix until thoroughly combined, stopping to scrape down the sides. Increase speed to high, and whip until soft peaks form (3–4 minutes). Pour filling into a prepared pie crust, and chill for 6–8 hours or until set.

You can build on this recipe in so many ways. I wanted to show you the base of it, and give you the freedom to dress it up how you want. Here are some ideas to try:

CRUST OPTIONS:

• Crushed Oreo crust

• Brownie base

• Hazelnut shortbread crust

ADDITIONAL OPTIONS:

• Melt Nutella, and pour a thin layer in the bottom of the crust before adding filling.

• Top with whipped cream, chopped hazelnuts, chocolate drizzle, or chocolate curls.

Mama's Famous Chocolate Pudding Pie

2 (3.4-ounce) boxes cook-and-serve chocolate pudding and pie filling

3½ cups whole milk

2 tablespoons butter

⅓ cup semisweet chocolate chips

2 (9-inch) pastry pie crusts, cooked and cooled)or use my recipe for Flaky Butter Pie Pastry on page 204)

Combine pudding mixes, milk, butter, and chocolate chips in a medium saucepan, and cook over medium heat until mixture comes to a boil; stir continually. Remove from heat; cool for 5 minutes, stirring twice. Pour filling into pie pastries, cool to room temperature, then cover and refrigerate. Serve with whipped cream.

NOTE:
Don't forget to let the pie cool to room temperature before refrigerating, or the pie may split or crack.

Mocha Fudge Pie
with Kahlúa and Starbucks

What do you get when you combine fudgy brownies with Kahlúa liqueur and Starbucks coffee? Complete and total awesomeness. And the best part? It's easy! You're going to look like a total rock star when you whip this pie out. And no one will ever know how ridiculously easy it is to prepare! Holla! Oh, and another plus? This freezes beautifully! The recipe makes two pies . . . one to eat now and one to throw in the freezer to wow your in-laws the next time they decide to show up unannounced.

½ cup Kahlúa (approximately), divided

1 serving Starbucks VIA Ready Brew

1 fudge brownie mix

Eggs and oil per brownie instructions

1½ cups milk

2 (3.9-ounce) boxes chocolate instant pudding mix

16 ounces frozen whipped topping, thawed, divided

NOTE:
Freeze UNCOVERED for several hours and THEN cover with aluminum foil or plastic wrap. This way, the pretty whipped topping keeps its pretty shape when frozen. Be sure to uncover it before you defrost it so it stays pretty.

Grease and flour bottom and sides of 2 (9-inch) deep-dish pie pans or a 9x13-inch baking dish. (Don't try to just spray with cooking spray, because that's what I did, and you should have seen how that turned out!) Mix 3 tablespoons Kahlúa with the Starbucks VIA Ready Brew (or 2 teaspoons instant coffee granules), and set aside to dissolve.

Mix brownie batter per instructions for fudgy brownies (not cake-like), substituting water with Kahlúa (usually ¼ cup). Divide batter evenly into pie pans; bake at 350° about 25 minutes or until just done. Cool completely.

Blend Kahlúa/coffee mixture and milk with an electric mixer. Add pudding mixes, and beat on low for 2 minutes. Fold in half of whipped topping. Spread pudding mixture evenly over both brownie pie crusts. Top pies with remaining whipped topping, cover, and refrigerate until ready to serve.

Chocolate Chip Pie

3 eggs

½ cup sugar

½ cup brown sugar

¼ cup corn syrup

¾ cup butter (1½ sticks), softened

1 teaspoon vanilla extract

⅓ teaspoon salt (a heaping ¼ teaspoon)

½ cup all-purpose flour

1 (12-ounce) package semisweet chocolate chips (about 2 cups)

1½ cups chopped nuts

2 (9-inch) pie shells (not deep dish)

Cream together eggs, sugars, corn syrup, butter, vanilla, and salt with an electric mixer until smooth. Add flour; mix until well combined. Stir in chocolate chips and nuts. Pour batter evenly into pie shells; bake at 325° for 45 minutes, or until a knife inserted halfway between edge and center comes out clean (it's okay if the center is still slightly jiggly).

NOTE:
Use the ready-made frozen pie shells or my recipe for Flaky Butter Pie Pastry (see page 204).

Mama's Apple Cider Pie

1 cup apple cider, plus more

¾ cup sugar

6–7 cups peeled, thick-sliced Granny Smith apples

2 tablespoons cornstarch

2 tablespoons water

¾ teaspoon cinnamon

1 tablespoon butter

2 (9-inch) deep-dish pie pastries

1 egg white, beaten

Combine apple cider and sugar in a large saucepan; bring to a boil. Reduce heat to medium high, add apples, and cook uncovered until apples are tender (about 8 minutes), stirring throughout cooking process. Drain syrup from apples into a 2-cup measuring pitcher. Add enough apple cider to syrup to measure 1⅓ cups liquid. Return syrup and apples to saucepan.

In a small bowl, combine cornstarch and water; stir well. Add cornstarch mixture and cinnamon to apples, and cook over medium-high heat until thickened, stirring constantly. Stir in butter. Spoon mixture into a pastry-lined, deep-dish pie plate. Cover with top crust, and seal edges. Cut 4–6 small slices into top crust to vent. Or get snazzy like Mama, and cut out decorative shapes. Brush crust with egg white, and bake at 375° for 45–50 minutes or until crust is golden brown.

NOTE:
Use the ready-made frozen pie shells or my recipe for Flaky Butter Pie Pastry (see page 204).

Mama's Apple Cider Pie

Fresh Strawberry Pie

¼ cup cornstarch

2 cups sugar

1 (3-ounce) package
   strawberry Jell-O

2 cups water

1 quart fresh strawberries

2 deep-dish pie pastries, baked
   and cooled

Whipped cream (optional)

Combine cornstarch, sugar, and strawberry Jell-O in a saucepan. Add water, and cook over medium heat, stirring constantly until mixtures thickens and coats back of a spoon. Cool mixture to room temperature, stirring occasionally.

Meanwhile, clean strawberries, and remove stems. Cut strawberries in half, and divide evenly into pie shells. Pour cooled strawberry glaze over strawberries. Cover, and refrigerate until ready to serve. Garnish with whipped cream, if desired.

Lemon Dream Pie

1 (14-ounce) can sweetened
   condensed milk

1 (8-ounce) block cream
   cheese, at room temperature

½ cup fresh lemon juice

Zest of 1 lemon

1 cup powdered sugar

1 (8-ounce) tub Cool Whip

2 (9-inch) graham cracker pie
   shells

Combine condensed milk and cream cheese, and beat with electric mixer on medium speed until smooth. Add lemon juice, zest, and powdered sugar; mix until blended. Fold in Cool Whip, and mix until just combined.

Divide mixture evenly into pie shells. Cover, and refrigerate 6 hours before serving. Store in refrigerator.

Coconut Cream Pie

- 1 (15-ounce) can cream of coconut
- 3 tablespoons milk
- 1 teaspoon coconut extract
- 1 (5.1-ounce) box vanilla instant pudding mix
- 1 (14-ounce) can sweetened condensed milk
- 2 cups sweetened flaked coconut
- 1 (8-ounce) tub Cool Whip, thawed
- 2 (9-inch) pie pastries, cooked and cooled

Add cream of coconut, milk, and coconut extract to a stand mixer or large bowl (using a handheld mixer), and mix on medium speed until smooth. Add pudding mix and condensed milk; mix until thoroughly combined. Fold in coconut and Cool Whip, and mix until just combined. Divide mixture evenly into pie shells. Cover, and refrigerate 6 hours before serving. Store in refrigerator.

NOTE:
Use the ready-made frozen pie shells or my recipe for Flaky Butter Pie Pastry (see page 204).

Show-Stopping Peach Cobbler

FILLING:

½ cup sugar

1 tablespoon cornstarch

Pinch of cinnamon

Pinch of salt

4 cups fresh peach slices

TOPPING:

1 cup all-purpose flour

2 tablespoons cornmeal

¼ cup plus 2 teaspoons sugar, divided

2 teaspoons baking powder

¼ teaspoon salt

4 tablespoons butter, melted

⅓ cup buttermilk

½ teaspoon vanilla extract

¼ teaspoon ground cinnamon

For Filling, combine sugar, cornstarch, cinnamon, and salt in a large bowl. Add peaches, and mix gently until evenly coated. Pour Filling into a 9x9-inch baking dish, and bake at 350° for 30 minutes. Remove peaches from oven, and increase temperature to 400°.

For Topping, combine flour, cornmeal, ¼ cup sugar, baking powder, and salt in a large bowl; mix well. Whisk melted butter, buttermilk, and vanilla together in small bowl; add to flour mixture, and mix until just combined. Spread Topping evenly over peaches. Combine cinnamon and remaining 2 teaspoons sugar in a small bowl; sprinkle over Topping. Bake 30 minutes at 400° or until filling is bubbly and top is golden brown.

Pumpkin Spice Cream Cheese Delight

1 cup all-purpose flour

½ cup butter, softened

1¼ cups chopped pecans

Pinch of salt

8 ounces cream cheese, softened

1 cup powdered sugar

16 ounces Cool Whip, divided

2 (3.4-ounce) boxes vanilla instant pudding mix

1½ cups milk

1 (15-ounce) can pumpkin

½ teaspoon pumpkin pie spice blend, plus more for sprinkling

Combine flour, butter, pecans, and salt; press into bottom of a 9x13-inch baking dish. Bake at 325° for 25 minutes. Cool completely. Mix cream cheese and powdered sugar with an electric mixer until smooth. Fold in half of Cool Whip; mix until combined. Spread cream cheese mixture evenly onto crust. Mix vanilla pudding mixes and milk with mixer until combined, then mix on medium speed for 1 more minute. Add pumpkin and pumpkin pie spice blend, and mix for 1 minute. Spread mixture evenly onto cream cheese layer. Spread remaining Cool Whip onto pumpkin layer; sprinkle with additional pumpkin pie spice.

Chocolate Éclair Dessert

2 sleeves graham crackers

2 (3.4-ounce) boxes French vanilla instant pudding mix

3¼ cups milk, divided

1 (8-ounce) container Cool Whip

1 cup sugar

½ cup cocoa powder

⅛ teaspoon salt

½ cup butter (1 stick)

1 teaspoon vanilla extract

Line bottom of 9x13-inch baking dish with whole graham crackers; set aside. Beat pudding mix and 3 cups milk together in large bowl with electric mixer until smooth and creamy. Fold in Cool Whip. Spread half of pudding mixture evenly over graham crackers. Arrange another layer of graham crackers over pudding layer. Spread remaining pudding mixture over graham crackers; arrange last layer of graham crackers on top of pudding layer. Cover, and refrigerate until icing is prepared.

Combine sugar, cocoa powder, salt, and butter in a small saucepan; bring to a boil over medium heat. Boil 1 minute; remove from heat. Stir in vanilla. Cool mixture, stirring occasionally, for 30 minutes. Pour over graham cracker layer. Cover, and refrigerate for 4 hours before serving. Store in refrigerator.

Chocolate Delight

1 cup all-purpose flour

½ cup butter, softened

1½ cups finely chopped pecans, divided

Pinch of salt

8 ounces cream cheese, softened

1 cup powdered sugar

16 ounces Cool Whip, divided

2 (3.9-ounce) boxes chocolate instant pudding mix

3 cups milk

Combine flour, butter, 1 cup pecans, and salt; press into bottom of 9x13-inch baking dish. Bake at 325° for 25 minutes. Cool completely. Mix cream cheese and powdered sugar with an electric mixer until smooth. Fold in half of Cool Whip; mix until combined. Spread cream cheese mixture evenly onto crust.

Mix pudding mixes and milk with an electric mixer on medium speed for 2 minutes. Spread chocolate mixture evenly onto cream cheese layer. Spread remaining Cool Whip onto chocolate layer; sprinkle with remaining pecans.

Blueberry Lush

1¾ cups graham cracker crumbs

¼ cup sugar

½ cup butter, at room temperature

8 ounces cream cheese, softened

1 cup powdered sugar

1 (8-ounce) container Cool Whip

1 (20-ounce) can blueberry pie filling

Combine graham cracker crumbs, sugar, and butter, and press into the bottom of a 9x13-inch baking dish; set aside. Mix cream cheese and powdered sugar with an electric mixer until smooth. Mix in Cool Whip until combined. Spread cream cheese mixture evenly onto graham cracker crust. Top with blueberry filling, cover, and refrigerate 4 hours before serving.

Black Forrest Trifle

2 (3.4-ounce) boxes chocolate instant pudding mix

3 cups milk

1 (15-ounce) chocolate pound cake (from the bakery)

¼ cup Kirsch (cherry liqueur)

1 (20-ounce) can cherry pie filling

1 (8-ounce) container Cool Whip

Beat pudding mixes and milk together in a large bowl with an electric mixer until smooth and creamy; set aside. Cut chocolate pound cake into 1-inch cubes; add to another large bowl. Drizzle Kirsch over cake pieces; add half of cake pieces to bottom of trifle dish or large glass bowl. Spread half of chocolate pudding over cake pieces. Spread half of Cool Whip over pudding. Spoon half of cherry pie filling over Cool Whip. Repeat layers. Cover, and refrigerate until ready to serve.

Tailgate Trifle

1 box angel food cake

1 (8-ounce) block cream cheese, softened

1 cup powdered sugar

1 (12-ounce) tub Cool Whip, thawed

1 (20-ounce) can cherry pie filling

Bake angel food cake per instructions, and cool cake completely. Cut cake into 1-inch cubes, and set aside. Beat cream cheese and powdered sugar with electric mixer until smooth. Fold in Cool Whip; set aside. To assemble, add half of angel food cake pieces to bottom of a trifle bowl (or any medium-large glass bowl). Cover angel food cake pieces with half of cream cheese mixture. Dollop half of the cherry pie filling onto cream cheese mixture. Repeat layers. Cover, and refrigerate until ready to serve.

TEAM COLOR OPTIONS:

Team Color—Pie Filling:

Blue—Blueberry

Red—Cherry

Purple—Blackberry

Garnet/Burgundy—Dark Cherry

Gold/Yellow—Pineapple

Orange—Peach

No-Churn Homemade Ice Cream

My neighbor (who I affectionately call Ninja Barb) and I sat in the front yard watching the neighborhood children play one Saturday afternoon while sampling this goodness, and we came up with about 437 flavor variations. I'll list a few below the recipe.

1 pint whipping cream

1 (14-ounce) can sweetened condensed milk

1 teaspoon vanilla extract

8 ounces ice cream topping of choice

With an electric mixer, whisk whipping cream on high speed until stiff peaks form. Fold in vanilla and condensed milk. Fold into a sealable container. Pour a few ribbons of ice cream topping over cream mixture; swirl with a spoon to incorporate it throughout. Freeze for 6–8 hours before serving.

FLAVOR VARIATIONS:

Banana Pudding: Add banana slices, crushed vanilla wafers, and marshmallow ice cream topping.

Butter Pecan: Substitute the vanilla with butter flavoring, and add chopped pecans.

Cookies and Cream: Add crushed Oreos and fudge ice cream topping.

Cherry Chocolate Chip: Substitute vanilla extract for almond; add cherry pie filling and mini chocolate chips.

Index

About the Author

Mandy Rivers, an accomplished cook and food blogger, has parlayed her outgoing personality and cooking acumen into an unexpected success story.

In college, Mandy worked at a bona fide honky tonk in the middle of the deep, deep South, sometimes helping in their short-order kitchen. Once she got her feet wet, that was all it took! She became so enchanted with cooking, she soon started adding her own creations to the menu. It was there she realized she'd found two of her dearest passions: cooking and feeding people.

To catalog her award-winning recipes, and as a creative outlet, Mandy quietly started a food blog that unexpectedly became wildly successful overnight—due to her delicious, approachable recipes and hilarious personality, www.southyourmouth.com.

The success of her blog was easily measured in the number of fans and followers on social media sites, like Pinterest, and it was there she caught the eye of the Food Network producers who were searching for the best cooks in America to star in the network series, *America's Best Cook*. Mandy was chosen to represent the South and compete in the premiere season of the latest sensation from Food Network.

Mandy's busy schedule includes a full-time job, marriage to "Husband," and three active children she calls her "onions." She enjoys creating new recipes and sharing them with family and friends. Mandy and her family live in Lexington, South Carolina.

Join Mandy now in her latest culinary accomplishment, *South Your Mouth!* Read her entertaining insights and amusing stories while enjoying recipes that are sure to become favorites and go-to dishes you will enjoy for years to come.